Close Quarter Productions in association with
John B Hobbs, Simon Oliver and Jermyn Street Theatre presents

THE HEART OF THINGS

by Giles Cole

The Heart of Things was first performed
on 10 March 2015 at the Jermyn Street Theatre, London.
It was subsequently performed at the Kenton Theatre,
Henley-on-Thames, in April 2015, by arrangement with
Kenton Theatre Presentations.

CAST

Brian Calder	**Ralph Watson**
Bob Farrow	**Keith Parry**
Peter Calder	**Nick Waring**
Ros Calder	**Patience Tomlinson**
Jacqui Price	**Amy Rockson**
William Farrow	**Ollo Clark**

PRODUCTION TEAM

Director	**Knight Mantell**
Set & Costume Design	**Joana Dias**
Lighting Design	**Nic Farman**
Sound Design	**Andrew Johnson**
Stage Manager	**Josephine Rossen**
Assistant Stage Manager	**Isabella Brain**
Chief Electrician /	
Show Operator	**Thom Collins**
Casting	**Georgia Fleury Reynolds**
Casting Consultant	**Lucy Casson**
Producers	**John B Hobbs**
	Alexander Marshall
	Giles Cole
Associate Producer	**Simon Oliver**

With grateful thanks to:

James Roose-Evans, Philip Talbot, Ruth Campbell, Jonathan Coutts, Anthony Brophy, David Philip and James Harman for their support and encouragement of this project; and Frontier Theatre Productions for rehearsal and audition space.

For more information about Close Quarter Productions please see the company website:

www.closequarter.net

R0444187903

R0444187903

CAST

Ralph Watson
Brian

Ralph Watson began work as an actor at Derby Playhouse in 1962.

Theatre credits have included: *The Hotel in Amsterdam* (Royal Court); *Close the Coalhouse Door* (Garrick); *The Brig* (Living Theatre of New York); *King Lear* and *Love's Labour's Lost* (Prospect Theatre). He also played in *Robin Hood* (Caird Co./ National Theatre); *Natural Inclinations* (Finborough); *Half Moon* (Southwark Playhouse, Battersea Arts Centre); *The Merchant of Venice* and *The Honest Whore* (Shakespeare's Globe); and *The School of Night* (Minerva Chichester).

His TV credits include: *Casualty*, *EastEnders*, *The Bill*, *London's Burning*, *Brookside*, *Doctor Who* and *Z-Cars*. He also worked in comedy classics such as *Dave Allen At Large*, *The Two Ronnies*, *To the Manor Born*, *The Fall and Rise of Reginald Perrin*, *Sykes*, *Porridge* and *Some Mothers Do 'Ave 'Em*.

Film credits include: *Shooting Fish*, *Reds*, *McVicar*, and *The Anniversary*.

Nick Waring
Peter

Recent theatre credits include: *Scared to Death*, *Taking Steps*, *Separate Tables*, *Strictly Murder*, *The Waiting Game*, *Framed*, *A Sentimental Journey* and *Room Service Included*. Other theatre includes: Romeo in *Romeo and Juliet*, D'Artagnan in *The Three Musketeers* and Konstantin in *The Seagull* – for which he was nominated for the Ian Charleson Award. West End includes Simon Bliss *in Hay Fever*, (Wyndhams); Backbite in *A School For Scandal*, Narrator in *Under Milk Wood* (Arts); Lord Alfred Douglas in *The Trials of Oscar Wilde* (Gielgud); *Star Quality* with Penelope Keith (Apollo); Sergeant Trotter in *The Mousetrap* and Caesar in *Antony and Cleopatra* with Vanessa Redgrave (World Tour). On No 1 tours he has played leads in *A Picture of Dorian Gray*, *The Importance of Being Earnest*, *A Doll's House*, *The Late Edwina Black* and ran around in a dress in *Charley's Aunt*. Nick was awarded the "star performer of the year" in 2009 for a tour of *The Business of Murder.*

Television credits include: *Endeavour, Breathless, Casualty, Dark Matters, Harry Enfield, Holby City, Doctors, London's Burning* and *Out of the Past.*

Film credits include: *Queen of the Desert* (2015); *When Saturday Comes Along, The Merchant of Venice, Big Pants.*

Patience Tomlinson
Ros

Patience was born and brought up in North Norfolk and is delighted to be doing this play, set in her native county. She trained at the Guildhall School of Music and Drama and has appeared in a wide variety of roles in theatres all over the country.

Theatre credits include: the National Theatre, the West End, the Young Vic and the Pleasance, where she played Mrs Gould in *Black 'ell* by Miles Malleson, part of the Forgotten Voices of the Great War season. Other stage roles include Annie in *The Norman Conquests*, Miss Skillen in *See How They Run*, The Abbess in *A Comedy of Errors*, and *she* has played both Cecily and (a little later) Miss Prism in *The Importance of Being Earnest.*

Hers is a well-known voice on BBC Radio 3 and 4 and she has made countless broadcasts of plays, poetry and short stories, including Isabelle Allende's novel *Paula* and Lady Mary Clive's *Christmas with the Savages* (both for Book at Bedtime); *Gal Audrey* by Audrey Whiting and *The Letters of Queen Victoria* (Woman's Hour); *Giving Up The Ghost* by Hilary Mantel (Book of the Week); and five *Tales of Victorian Norfolk* by Mary Mann (Afternoon Story). Patience has recorded nearly 200 audio books, including *Charles Dickens, A Life* by Claire Tomalin, *Wives and Daughters* by Elizabeth Gaskell, *Millions Like Us* by Virginia Nicholson, *A Glass of Blessings* by Barbara Pym, and *Time to be in Earnest*, the autobiography by PD James.

Television credits include: *The Day Today, Friday Night Armistice, In the Red* and *Shadowplay*. Patience has written and performs a one-woman show called *A Tale That Is Told* about the brilliant Victorian Norfolk novelist and short story writer, Mary E Mann.

Keith Parry
Bob

Recent theatre work includes: the role of Fred Voles in *Summer Day's Dream* at the Finborough. Other roles include Davies in *The Caretaker* and Arthur Birling in *An Inspector Calls* for the Horseshoe Theatre Co, Cambridge, Alfieri in *A View from the Bridge* and Ross, Bishop How and Snork in *The Elephant Man* for the Broadway Theatre, Catford. Keith's classical experience, primarily off London fringe, is extensive, having played many significant roles including Shylock, King Lear and Falstaff.

TV & Film credits include: *Dr Who*, *EastEnders* and *Doctors* for the BBC and *The Jury* for ITV. Keith also contributed to several award-winning short and feature length films including *The Drummond Will*, *Stranger Things*, *Waiting for a Stranger* and *Journey Home*.

His professional acting career started late in life but he has rapidly built up a portfolio of film, TV and theatre credits. He was born in the West Midlands and is a keen supporter of West Bromwich Albion FC. When not acting he keeps tropical fish and enjoys a spot of DIY.

Amy Rockson
Jacqui

Amy trained at the Mountview Academy of Theatre Arts.

Theatre credits include: Elvira in *Blithe Spirit* (York Theatre Royal); Mickey in *The Odd Couple* (Horse Cross Arts Theatre); Titania/ Hippolyta in *A Midsummer Night's Dream* (Shakespeare at the Tobacco Factory); Lady Sneerwell in *The School for Scandal*, Devil/Pride/Duchess of Vanholt in *Doctor Faustus* (Greenwich Theatre); Emma in *Funny Girl* (Chichester Festival Theatre); Dr Pinch's Assistant in *The Comedy of Errors* (RSC); Adele in *Under Pressure* (Jermyn Street); Betty Dullfeet/Dockdaisy in *The Resistible Rise of Arturo Ui*, Jessica Brandon in *Henry VIII* (Bridewell); *Oedipus, Agamemnon, Androcles and the Lion*

(Scoop Amphitheatre); Tolla in *Made in Spain* (Etcetera); Angel in *If I Should Fall* (Off Broadway Theatre); Daria in *Six Geese A Laying* (Soho Theatre); *Cinderella* (Oxford Playhouse).

Television credits include: *Holby City* and *Doctors*.

Film credits include: *London Voodoo, Panchreston, Going Nowhere.*

Amy plays the role of Zoe Crick in the award-winning game, *Zombies,Run!*

Ollo Clark
William

Ollo finished his training at LAMDA in August 2014, and before that read English at Oxford University. He represented LAMDA at the Shakespeare's Globe Sam Wanamaker Festival in 2014, and is a performer and producer for ONEOHONE Theatre Company.

His credits during training include: Lee in *Vera, Vera, Vera*, Ferdinand in *The Duchess of Malfi*, Macbeth in *Macbeth* and Tom Fashion in *A Trip to Scarborough*. Since leaving LAMDA he played Charlie Dalton in *Secret Cinema Presents Dead Poets Society* and the Son in *My Dad's Gap Year*.

He has appeared in three short films: *FLAT, A Viewfinder* and *Get Lucky/Chasing Dragons*.

PRODUCTION TEAM

Knight Mantell
Director

A graduate of Manchester University's drama department, Knight has more than 40 years' experience as actor, director, writer and theatre producer. He has played opposite Alec Guinness, Maggie Smith, Alastair Sim, Topol, Margaret Leighton, Gary Wilmot and John Inman in many parts ranging from Dracula to Archie Rice, Salieri to Widow Twankey. He has toured with *Equus, The Canterbury Tales* and as Cardinal Richelieu in *The Three Musketeers*.

Most recently he directed the acclaimed production of *The Art of Concealment*, both at Jermyn Street Theatre and Riverside Studios, and *The White Carnation* at the Finborough and Jermyn Street Theatres. He was founder director of Channel Theatre Company and Lyceum Productions, mounting productions of *Thérèse Raquin, The Norman Conquests, Everyman* and *Don Juan in Hell*. He has directed opera in Hong Kong. Work with the British Actors Theatre Company includes *Coupler in The Relapse* as well as directing *The Dresser* with Ian Lavender, and *The Rivals*. He has directed *Love's Labour's Lost* and *The Comedy of Errors*, and toured in *Journey's End* and as Dr Willis in *The Madness of George III* with Simon Ward, as well as playing Jacob in Strindberg's *The Apartment*.

Television work includes: *Lillie, Dempsey and Makepeace, Martin Chuzzlewitt* and *Game On*.

Film work includes: *The Fool* with Derek Jacobi and *Wild Justice* with Roy Scheider.

Giles Cole
Writer/Co-producer

Giles is a writer and producer, who set up Close Quarter Productions with Sandy Marshall and former BBC producer John B Hobbs four years ago. Giles is also the chairman of Frontier Theatre Productions, founded in 2013 by James Roose-Evans, where the emphasis is on older performers and theatre professionals working in tandem with younger ones, and bridging the creative gulf; and he is a founder member and newsletter editor of the Terence Rattigan Society.

www.closequarter.net
www.frontiertheatreproductions.co.uk
www.theterencerattigansociety.co.uk

Alexander 'Sandy' Marshall
Producer

Sandy is the American end of the Close Quarter Production team. In the past five years Close Quarter have produced twenty shows in the UK and/or USA including *The Art of Concealment* (about the life of Terence Rattigan) which played to sold-out houses and four and five-star reviews in London – first at the Jermyn Street Theatre and later at Riverside Studios. Off-Broadway Close Quarter produced, and Marshall directed, *Max Maven Thinking In Person* and *Jadoo* to unanimous raves. In the UK they produced and Marshall wrote and directed *AND IN THE END: The Death and Life of John Lennon* (also at Jermyn Street Theatre). In the Windy City of Chicago, Close Quarter produced several plays including *Short Guys With Glasses, Bending Minds & Bending Dreams, Seeing With the Mind's Eye* and *Fooling Buddha* (the latter two also directed by Marshall).

Sandy is a two-time Emmy® Award winner (seven nominations); who has also won the Golden Eagle, Gold Medal at the New York Film and Television Festival and the Benjamin Franklin Award for his epic biography about his legendary magician father, *Beating a Dead Horse: The Life and Times of Jay Marshall.*

Fifty years in show business has not dulled his enthusiasm to find the truth that hides in the darkened corners of his craft. Sandy lives in the Chelsea section of New York City with his talented wife, singer/songwriter Susan Palmer Marshall and their two ginger cats, Macallister and Macgregor.

www.alexandersandymarshall.com

John B Hobbs
Producer

John has had a distinguished career as producer and director for BBC Television.

Directing credits include: *Clochemerle, Butterflies, Roger Doesn't Live Here Anymore, Pinkerton's Progress, Leaving, Alas Smith and Jones, Three Up Two Down, Brush Strokes, Bread, 'Allo 'Allo* and *Mulberry.* His series *Lame Ducks*, starring John Duttine, Brian Murphy and Lorraine Chase, achieved the highest viewing figures known for comedy on BBC2.

His work in the theatre encompasses writing, directing and producing. For the Mill at Sonning he has directed *The Bed Before Yesterday, Spring and Port Wine, Dames at Sea, Charley's Aunt* and the world premiere of *The Making of Julia.* For the Grand Theatre Swansea his productions include *Wife Begins at Forty* and *One for the Road.* In the 1990s he directed a UK tour of *Same Time Next Year,* a national tour of *Happy as a Sandbag* and Jimmy Perry's *That's Showbiz!* at the Wimbledon Theatre. Other stage credits include directing Ray Cooney's *Out of Order* and producing and directing *Business Affairs* by John Chapman and Jeremy Lloyd.

John also directed the feature film *La Passione* starring Shirley Bassey and produced by Warner Bros and Fugitive Films, with screenplay and music by Chris Rea.

Joana Dias
Set and Costume Design

Joana graduated from Central School of Speech and Drama (CSSD) with a BA in Design for Stage in 2012.

Design work includes: *Christmas* by Simon Stephens (White Bear Theatre, Kennington); *MOJO* (White Bear Theatre); *The Apple Tree* (Ye Olde Rose and Crown, Walthamstow); *Flowers of the Field* (White Bear Theatre); *Idylls of the King* (assistant designer, Oxford Playhouse); *How To Succeed In Business Without Really Trying* (Ye Olde Rose And Crown); *The Seagull* by Anton Chekhov (White Bear Theatre); *Carmen* (King's Head Theatre, Islington); *As I Lay Dying* by William Faulkner, devised performance (Webber Douglas Studio, Central School of Speech and Drama); *Seventh Continent*, a site-specific performance directed by Julian Maynard Smith (Brixton Market).

Film work includes: *Greater Things*, a feature film directed by Vahid

Hakimzadeh, *Long Forgotten Films*, directed by Jon Stanford, *Forever Autumn*, a Gary Barlow music video, *Karma*, a Snoop Dogg music video featuring Outlawz and *Never Been In Love*, a Dave Stewart music video featuring Charlotte Carter-Allen.

Nic Farman
Lighting Design

Nic is the winner of the Francis Reid Award as part of the ALD Michael Northen Bursary 2013.

Lighting Design credits include: *Dracula!* (*Mr Swallow The Musical*) (Soho Theatre); *Macbeth* (LOST Theatre); *Pig Girl, The Immortal Hour, Hostage Song, Valley of Song* (Finborough Theatre); *Empires* (Bush Theatre, Radar Festival); *Romeo and Juliet; Still the Beating of my Heart, Blood Wedding, Mac-Beth, Last of the Red Hot Lovers, The Woyzeck* (National Tour); *Richard III* (Cockpit Theatre, Marlborough College, Greenwich Theatre); *The Little Mermaid* (Riverside Studios); *The Bald Prima Donna; The Upstanding Member* (Old Red Lion Theatre); *The Blind/The Intruder* (Old Red Lion Theatre, transfer to The Tabard); *The Mobile Phone Show* (Deafinitely Theatre); *Cinderella* (Leicester Square Theatre); *Fulfil Me Fully, Phil; A Life in Monochrome* (The Space); *Twelfth Night* (The Courtyard); *The Laramie Project* (Leicester Curve).

Associate/Assistant Lighting Design credits include: *Phenomenal People* (FUEL); *The White Carnation* (Jermyn Street Theatre); *Sixty-Six Books* (Bush Theatre).

Andrew Johnson
Sound Design

In a career spanning over 30 years, Andrew has worked as a freelance sound designer, music producer and engineer with artists ranging from Status Quo to Ray Charles, and on a diverse range of theatrical and corporate productions in venues around the world, from the Royal Albert Hall in London to a monastery in Venice and a medieval shipyard in Barcelona. In 2012 he worked *with* the Royal Theatrical Fund, in charge of designing and operating the sound for their production of *Dickens and the Actors* at London's Guildhall, to mark the Queen's Diamond Jubilee and the bicentenary of Dickens' birth. He has his own sound studio in Sussex.

Josephine Rossen

Stage Manager

Josephine graduated from Middlesex University in 2012 with a degree in Theatre Arts.

Theatre credits include: Assistant Stage Manager for Madeleine Bowyer's *Fragile* at the Cockpit Theatre (2013); Stage Manager for Front Foot Theatre's production of *The Seagull* at The White Bear (2013); Deputy Stage Manager for Paper Birds' preview of *Broke* at the Greenwich Theatre (2014); and Stage Manager for Aria Entertainment's revival of *Free As Air* at the Finborough Theatre (2014).

Opera credits include: Stage Manager and Assistant Director for Winslow Hall Opera's *Le Nozze Di Figaro* in 2012 and *Carmen* in 2013, and working as Stage Manager for Gestalt Arts' *Clive and Other Stories* at the Peckham Asylum in 2014.

Josephine's most recent work includes working as Stage Manager for The Company Arts' production of *The Three Sisters* at the Cockpit Theatre (2015) and Deputy Stage Manager for Up In Arms' production of *Visitors* at The Bush Theatre (2014/15) which won the Critics' Circle Theatre Award for most promising playwright.

Isabella Brain

Assistant Stage Manager

Isabella graduated from LAMDA's technical course in 2014 and has since worked as Stage Manager for *Virgins Die Horny* at the Courtyard Theatre and *Warehouse of Dreams* at the Lion and Unicorn Theatre; she was Deputy Stage Manager for *Ragtime: The Musical* at The Pleasance Theatre, and Assistant Stage Manager for *A Christmas Carol*. Her work experience also includes stage managing *Sherlock Holmes* at The Pleasance and being Assistant Stage Manager on *Uncle Vanya* at The Print Room.

CLOSE QUARTER
PRODUCTIONS

Close Quarter Productions Ltd (newly named in 2014) began life in Brighton in 2011 with the first production of *The Art of Concealment: The Life of Terence Rattigan* by Giles Cole, directed by Tom Latter. It was specially written for the Rattigan centenary year and, following its success in Brighton, a new production was then mounted at the Jermyn Street Theatre the following year, directed by Knight Mantell, which received glowing reviews and subsequently transferred to Riverside Studios, with a substantially new cast. *And in the End – The Death and Life of John Lennon*, written and directed by Alexander Marshall was presented at Jermyn Street Theatre in 2013, having previously been seen at the Edinburgh Festival and in Australia.

Close Quarter Productions is a co-operative venture bringing together writers, actors, directors and designers. The aims and objectives are to present new and exciting work in smaller scale venues, with the emphasis on creating opportunities for both younger and older performers working together to develop imaginative, perceptive and challenging theatre. And this includes shows devoted to the art of magic.

In development is *The Loves of Ida Rubinstein*, a play inspired by the book *Dancing in the Vortex* by Vicki Woolf: Paris, 1908. Ida Rubinstein, a 23-year-old Russian Jewish aristocrat, is planning to appear naked in the ballet Salomé. Her brother-in-law commits her to an asylum to prevent such disgrace. Her fearsome Russian aunt arranges her release and she becomes a sensation both on and off stage. Fifty years later she has retreated from the world that adored her and is living as a recluse. *The Loves of Ida Rubinstein* is a meditation on love, age and the shallowness of fame, seen through the eyes of an ageing woman haunted by the ghosts of her extraordinary past.

www.closequarter.net

JERMYN STREET THEATRE

During the 1930s the basement of 16b Jermyn Street was home to the glamorous Monseigneur Restaurant and Club. The space was converted into a theatre by Howard Jameson and Penny Horner in the early 1990s, and Jermyn Street Theatre staged its first production in August 1994. Over the last twenty years the theatre has established itself as one of London's leading Off-West End studio theatres.

Gene David Kirk became Artistic Director in 2009. With his Associate Director Anthony Biggs he was instrumental in transforming the theatre's creative output with a number of critically acclaimed revivals of rarely performed plays including Charles Morgan's post-war classic *The River Line*, the UK premiere of Ibsen's first performed play *St John's Night* with Olivier-winning actress Sarah Crowe, and another Ibsen: his rarely performed late play *Little Eyolf* starring Imogen Stubbs and Doreen Mantle.

Other notable successes include 70's musical *Boy Meets Boy*, which was nominated for six Off-West End Awards, *The Two Character Play* by Tennessee Williams, Graham Greene's *The Living Room* and the Ivor Novello musical *Gay's The Word*. In 2012 Trevor Nunn directed the World Premiere of Samuel Beckett's radio play *All That Fall* starring Eileen Atkins and Michael Gambon. The production subsequently transferred to the West End's Arts Theatre and then to New York's 59E59 Theatre.

Anthony Biggs became Artistic Director in 2013 and has continued the policy of staging rediscovered classic plays alongside new plays and musicals. Recent revivals include Frederick Lonsdale's 1920's comedy of manners *On Approval*, David Pinner's 1970's comedy *The Potsdam Quartet*, and R.C. Sherriff's *The White Carnation*. New work includes a season of Steven Berkoff's hard-hitting one act plays entitled *Religion and Anarchy* and the premiere of the musical *Return of the Soldier* based on the First World War novel by Rebecca West. This summer Anthony produced a critically-acclaimed South African Season with sixteen productions of plays by SA writers including Athol Fugard and Reza De Wet.

Jermyn Street Theatre was nominated for the Peter Brook Empty Space Award in 2011 and won the Stage 100 Best Fringe Theatre in 2012. Jermyn Street Theatre is a registered charity and receives no public subsidy.

Chairman: Howard Jameson
General Manager: Penny Horner
Artistic Director: Anthony Biggs
Chief Electrician: Thom Collins
With thanks to all the Jermyn Street Theatre volunteers.

www.jermynstreettheatre.co.uk

THE HEART OF THINGS

Giles Cole

THE HEART OF THINGS

OBERON BOOKS
LONDON

WWW.OBERONBOOKS.COM

First published in 2015 by Oberon Books Ltd
521 Caledonian Road, London N7 9RH
Tel: +44 (0) 20 7607 3637 / Fax: +44 (0) 20 7607 3629
e-mail: info@oberonbooks.com
www.oberonbooks.com

A catalogue record for this book is available from the British
Library.

PB ISBN: 978-1-78319-866-5
E ISBN: 978-1-78319-867-2

Graphic design by Clare Martin

Printed, bound and converted
by CPI Group (UK) Ltd, Croydon, CR0 4YY.

Visit www.oberonbooks.com to read more about all our books
and to buy them. You will also find features, author interviews and
news of any author events, and you can sign up for e-newsletters
so that you're always first to hear about our new releases.

Characters

BRIAN CALDER
(75-81)

PETER CALDER
(his son, 41-47)

ROS CALDER
(his daughter, 44-50)

JACQUI PRICE
(42)

BOB FARROW
(51-57)

WILLIAM FARROW
(Ros and Bob's son, 23)

Setting
The kitchen of a house in a village near the Norfolk coast.

Timescale
May 2004 and May 2010.

Note
The music indicated at the end of scenes is not obligatory but, if incorporated, it is suggested that it be taken from Mozart's Piano Concerto No. 23 in A major *(2nd movement: Adagio)* and the Piano Concerto No. 24 in C minor *(2nd movement: Larghetto).*

ACT ONE

SCENE ONE

Apart from the usual kitchen features, sink, cooker, fridge, there is an old-fashioned wooden table where food is both prepared and eaten, an old comfortable armchair and a door to the garden. There is also a door or archway leading to the hallway and the rest of the house. A crate of beer is visible in one corner of the kitchen. The overall feel is of a living space where little has changed since the family moved in thirty-five years ago. It's functional, clean, but jaded.

Music. A projection on the back wall fades up: Saturday 8 May, 2004.

The projection disappears. Lights up on BOB, aged fifty-one, sturdily-built, wearing a shabby sweater and jeans, who is sitting at the kitchen table building a model boat out of matchsticks and balsa wood with great concentration. It is about two-thirds complete. The table also contains a few plates from lunch earlier. BOB has a pronounced Norfolk accent.

BRIAN, a still-vigorous man of seventy-five, but confined to a wheelchair, is watching BOB. Unlike BOB, he is not a local man, originally being from South-East London. He has a bottle of beer to hand. Music fades.

BRIAN: You ever going to finish that thing?

    Pause.

    Twenty years to build one little boat! *(Laughs.)* Beats me how you've got the patience.

BOB: Fifteen year.

BRIAN: Fifteen, twenty, what's the difference? You could build a real one quicker than that. Several real ones.

    A beat. BOB adds another piece, very carefully. A car is heard arriving. Car doors opening and closing.

BOB: Always liked boats.

BRIAN: You don't say.

BOB: When I were a boy I used to watch the coastal traders.
Down by the harbour. All had names ending in ITY.
The Amity, the Austerity, the Aseity – whatever that means.

BRIAN: Don't ask me. Peter's the one to ask for a thing like
that. Seeing as he's gracing us with his presence for once.
(A beat.) Is that my paper you're using?

BOB: I don' know. Jus' found it on the table.

BRIAN: I haven't read today's paper yet.

BOB: Sorry, Brian.

BOB carefully lifts up his boat and slides the Daily Mirror *out from
under it. BRIAN takes it, starts to read it.*

Di'n't want to get glue on Ros's table. Di'n't think she'd be
best pleased.

BRIAN: She's not the sole proprietor of the furniture in this
house, y'know.

*BOB looks around in search of another paper he can use, opens a
drawer in the kitchen table, takes out some paper napkins and unfolds
two of them. Puts the boat on top of them.*

BOB: We going to celebrate Ros's birthday tomorrow then?

BRIAN: *(Still reading.)* We'll have a drink or two, I dare say.

BOB: Thought I might take her out for a bit of a meal. A treat,
like. Somethin' a bit special. *(No further reaction from BRIAN.)*
Thought we could go into Yarmouth. Nice bit of steak.

BRIAN: She doesn't need to go out for meals. Doesn't need
that kind of fuss.

*PETER enters from the garden door, carrying two bottles of white
wine and an overnight bag. He is forty-one years old, slightly built,
not exactly handsome, but neat of appearance. He wears a jacket,
cords, sensible shoes and spectacles.*

BOB: Hello, Peter.

PETER: Bob. Still busy shipbuilding?

BOB: Can't rush it.

PETER puts his bag down on a chair, deposits the wine on the table.

PETER: Indeed not. *(Nods at BRIAN.)* All right, Dad?
How are we?

BRIAN: I'm still here. As you can see.

He goes back to his paper. PETER exchanges a look with BOB.

PETER: Same old cheerful soul.

BOB: I were tellin' Brian, Peter, that when I were a lad I used
to watch all the coastal traders with names endin' in ITY.

PETER: Uhuh.

BOB: Aseity. Wha's that mean then?

PETER: Aseity? The state of being by, or from, itself.
Or oneself. Latin 'a se' – from oneself.

BOB: Oh, right. Never did Latin at school.

PETER: No, it's been unfashionable for quite some time.
Is Ros around?

BOB: Oh yes. She's doin' a spot o' dustin'.

PETER: Ah. So, how have you been, Bob?

BOB: Fair to middlin'. *(Pause.)* William's gettin' on well.

PETER: Good, good. Bright lad.

BOB: Oh yes.

PETER: How often do you see him these days?

BOB: Every week or two. He's a good boy. Always got time for
his old dad.

BRIAN folds up the Mirror *noisily and very pointedly starts to wheel
himself out to the hallway.*

A' right, Brian?

BRIAN: Going to see what's on telly.

BRIAN goes. BOB looks at PETER for some kind of reaction to BRIAN's leaving.

BOB: Still not talkin', you two?

PETER: I've come to the conclusion, Bob, after all these years, that our not talking is actually a sign of affection.

BOB: *(Uncertain of PETER's tone.)* Oh. Right.

ROS and BRIAN are heard in the hallway.

ROS: *(Off.)* Everything all right, Dad?

BRIAN: *(Off.)* Your brother's arrived.

ROS: *(Off.)* Oh! Lovely.

ROS appears from the hallway. ROS is a woman of forty-four, who gives the impression of not worrying too much about her appearance. She wears an apron over a loose dress and unlike PETER, she has a slight Norfolk accent. She removes the apron as she comes in.

ROS: Petey – there you are! How lovely.

She gives him a quick hug and a kiss.

Sorry, I've been doing a bit of tidying. Good drive?

PETER: Not too bad.

The sound of the TV can be heard, faintly, as BRIAN flicks through the channels.

ROS: It's a beautiful day. You two boys ought to go and stretch your legs.

PETER: So we're 'the two boys' now, are we?

ROS: Nice to see you're keeping each other company.

BOB: Had a good old mardle, Ros. Bit of a Latin lesson.

ROS: Really?

BOB: Learned the meaning of that word – what was it?

PETER: Aseity. The state of being on one's own. A state of existence derived entirely from oneself. Would that it were possible.

ROS gives him a look.

ROS: Bob, why don't you go and keep Dad company for five minutes? Let me have a little gossip and a catch-up with Peter.

BOB: Right. I'll go an' see what the old boy's watchin' on the telly. Do you keep an eye on the boat for me.

He goes.

PETER: Keep an eye on the boat? Who does he think is going to steal it?

ROS puts the kettle on to make tea.

ROS: It keeps him happy.

PETER: He ought to be helping you out.

ROS: Don't start, Petey.

PETER: Well, he should. Sitting about making matchstick models. There's all sorts to get done, I'm sure.

ROS: Tea?

PETER: I'll do it.

PETER takes mugs from a rack. Suddenly remembers something, takes a small package from his jacket pocket.

I know your birthday's not till tomorrow, but you might as well have this now. *(Hands her the package.)* It's only earrings.

ROS: *(Opening it.)* Lovely, Petey. Thank you. That's very sweet of you.

Gives him a kiss. She puts the earrings on and disposes of the paper in the kitchen bin.

How do they look?

PETER smiles approvingly, nods.

PETER: Great. They suit you.

ROS: Oh, Petey, don't. I know I look awful these days. Old before my time. That's what they say.

PETER: That's what who says?

ROS: Oh…people. You know. *(Changing tack.)* I've got to start supper soon. Thought I'd make a shepherd's pie, is that all right?

PETER: Sure. Whatever.

ROS: It's quick and easy. And Bob likes it.

PETER: Are you turning into a little wifey again?

ROS: Don't be like that. No, Bob and I aren't like that any more. He's just here for my birthday weekend. Felt I had to ask him.

PETER: He's been building that model boat for as long as I can remember.

ROS: To be honest I'm sick of the sight of the blessed thing. Teabags.

PETER finds the tea caddy, puts teabags in the mugs.

PETER: William back yet?

ROS: He'll be back later. He's going to a disco with some schoolfriends.

PETER: Those were the days. So how are things with dear old Bob?

ROS: You know how it is, Peter. He's a good man at heart.

PETER: Mm? But?

ROS: He tries to be a good father to William, but William's so independent now, he feels rather out of it. That's why I try to include him in birthdays and things. Have him round for a meal now and then.

PETER: I meant how are things with Bob and *you*.

ROS: Well, I try to be friendly, for William's sake, but well, I just can't feel the same way any more.

PETER: You never were exactly the love-match of the century, were you?

ROS: *(A beat.)* No. But I've got William.

PETER gives her shoulders a quick squeeze.

PETER: Oh yes. Indeed.

ROS: I do worry about you, though.

The kettle has boiled. ROS pours water into the mugs.

PETER: *(Deciding to pursue this.)* Why's that?

ROS: Well, you're the one who's had every opportunity, Peter, and you seem determined to…ohhh… *(Waves her hand in a vague, dismissive gesture.)*.

PETER: Go on. Determined to what?

ROS: It doesn't matter.

PETER: No. Go on. Say what you were going to say.

ROS: Well… *(A beat.)* You know what I think –

PETER: No, I don't. Why would I know what you think?

Pause.

ROS: Well, there you are, in London, right in the heart of things, surrounded by…by colleagues, and friends, and… and you never seem to be able to make anything of it.

Of yourself. We're not youngsters any more, Peter. We're supposed to be in the prime of our lives. Well, way past our prime in my case.

PETER: Haven't been here five minutes and already I'm getting a lecture.

ROS: I don't mean it like that, you know I don't.

PETER moves a few paces away, fiddles with a saucepan lid that is sitting on the work surface.

I mean, I've no idea what sort of things you like these days. Do you still like Chinese takeaways? Do you still sit for hours with your nose in a book, or do you go for walks? Is there anywhere to walk where you live?

PETER: There's the Common.

ROS: Oh yes, Clapham Common. We went to a party near there when we were teenagers – do you remember? – in the days when we used to go down to London. They were awful, those parties. Standing about in people's kitchens with the floor all sticky from cheap beer and people getting off with each other in every corner, and me afraid to do anything because you were there. They must've thought we were a right pair. A brother and sister going to parties together and always the last two standing. God, it makes me shudder just to think about it. But it seemed magical at the time. Didn't it? To us. Just to be away from here. Bleak House you used to call it, here. Do you remember?

PETER nods.

Do you still go to parties? Well, they'd be more grown up parties, wouldn't they? Dinner parties. I bet there are hundreds of dinner parties every night in Clapham. Hundreds of people sitting round their smart dining tables, and talking about politics and whatnot. Is that what it's like? Peter? Do you go to parties like that?

PETER: No.

ROS: Never?

PETER: Hardly ever. Last one I went to the entire evening was spent talking about the latest evictions on *Big Brother*. It was like being at a seminar on the futility of existence. I smiled a lot and got rather drunk.

ROS: I quite like *Big Brother*.

PETER: Oh dear.

ROS: What else do you do, Petey? Tell me more about you. I like it when you tell me things.

PETER: My life is hardly very exciting, Ros. Mostly I go to work every day and try and write in the evenings. When I can.

ROS: Oh – yes. Any news on the book?

PETER: Sadly not.

ROS: No interest at all?

PETER: Not a dicky bird.

ROS: There are always others. Other publishers.

PETER: Oh yes. And I intend to try them all. The battle continues. We are not down-hearted! Don't tell Dad, though. The disappointment might kill him.

ROS: It'll happen, Petey, I'm sure it will. You're clever, you have opinions, you – oh, do put that saucepan lid down, it's driving me nuts…

Pause. He carefully replaces the saucepan lid.

I'm sorry. I'm a bit on edge. I don't normally rattle on like this. Sorry. It's good to see you.

A beat. ROS smiles.

How's Harry?

PETER: He's…quite a high flyer these days. Doesn't spend much time at the house. Always off on some business trip or other.

ROS: At least you've still got the rent coming in.

PETER: Well, mortgage. Yes.

ROS: Still, it's good to have that to rely on. Be tricky on your own, otherwise, I expect.

PETER: Oh yes. Couldn't manage it on my own.

A small silence. ROS looks at him, fondly.

ROS: For heaven's sake take them that tea before it gets cold.

PETER: Yup. Right.

She passes him a carton of milk. He pours milk into each mug and puts two of them on a tray.

BRIAN appears from the hallway. BOB is pushing the wheelchair.

ROS: Petey was just bringing you a cup of tea.

BRIAN: This is no time for tea.

PETER: *(Elaborately patient.)* OK. No tea it is. Bob?

BOB: *(Unsure whether to follow suit.)* Er…

PETER: There's no compulsion.

BOB: Right. *(A beat.)* I'm fine, thanks.

PETER: No teas all round then.

PETER puts the tray by the sink.

BRIAN wheels himself to the beer crate in the corner and takes a bottle, opens it with an opener he keeps tied to a piece of string on his belt.

ROS: Anything good on the telly?

BRIAN: No.

BOB: Might watch the news later. We like the news, don't we, Brian? Always like the news.

BRIAN inspects one of the bottles of wine on the table.

BRIAN: Good wine?

PETER: Purely Fussy. That's what we smart Londoners call Pouilly Fuissé.

BRIAN: Is it now? I seem to remember you made the same crack last time you graced us with your presence.

ROS: Now, Dad…

PETER: My apologies. I'll try not to say it again next time.

He puts the wine in the fridge.

BRIAN: You can come home more than once a year, y'know. Not just for your sister's birthday.

PETER: I know.

BRIAN: My birthday, for instance. You could have come home for that.

PETER: You could have invited me.

BRIAN: There was no special do. Even though I turned seventy-five.

ROS: Please! I want this to be a nice weekend.

BRIAN: Not much to ask. A bit of conversation with your own son.

ROS looks at him, then turns and leaves.

ROS: Come along, Bob. Leave them to it for a minute.
I think they're warming up for one of their ding-dongs.

BOB: Right.

BOB follows ROS out to the hallway.

BRIAN and PETER regard each other warily.

PETER: Let's have a conversation then.

BRIAN: So. What's happened in your life in the last year? Any news?

PETER: Not to speak of, no.

BRIAN: Well, that's a fine bloody start. No news in a whole year?

PETER: Not what you'd call news. Just…trivial stuff.

BRIAN: Tell me some trivial stuff then.

Pause. PETER decides to make an effort at this.

PETER: I've been to a couple of dinner parties. Not very interesting. I'm still working on my book. I go to concerts. Occasionally. But I'm not what you'd call a classical music buff. I just enjoy live music. The sound of a proper orchestra. It sort of – well, you'll laugh, but I always think it sort of cleanses the soul.

BRIAN: Cleanses the soul, eh?

PETER: In a manner of speaking.

BRIAN: Not a manner of speaking I understand.

PETER: Perhaps not.

BRIAN: Who's your favourite?

PETER: Sorry?

BRIAN: Composer.

PETER: Well, I'm rather fond of Mozart, actually.

BRIAN: Ah. Mozart.

PETER: Yes. Particularly the piano concertos and Symphony number 40. In G Minor.

BRIAN: G Minor, eh?

PETER: Yes. It happens to be written in G Minor.

BRIAN: I thought you said you weren't a music buff.

PETER: I'm not. Knowing that a symphony happens to be written in a certain key is hardly being an expert. Anyway, it's a very well-known symphony. Everybody knows it.

BRIAN: I don't know it.

PETER: You might if you heard it.

BRIAN: How could I know it if I heard it?

PETER: I mean you might realise that you had heard it before.

BRIAN: I don't listen to Mozart. Ever. Mozart isn't for the likes of me.

PETER: Might be, if you gave it a chance.

BRIAN: Prefer a nice tune myself. Something you can hum along to.

PETER: The Beach Boys, yes. I remember.

BRIAN: Nothing wrong with The Beach Boys.

PETER: Have you been listening to The Beach Boys all year then? Or have you still been keeping the house in respectful silence?

ROS comes back in.

ROS: Sorry, I've got to start on the potatoes.

BRIAN: We've been talking about Mozart.

ROS: Really? That's not like you.

BRIAN: That's what I keep trying to tell your brother.

ROS starts to peel potatoes at the sink.

BOB reappears, again following ROS.

(To PETER.) Any other news from the great metropolis, then?

PETER: Not really, no.

BRIAN: My God, if your mother could hear you now! You've never had much to say for yourself, have you? Always the little boy lost. Not a clue what life's about, despite all your education. Your mother knew that, and it broke her heart –

PETER: That simply isn't true! You make it up, Dad, to suit your own distorted view of things.

BRIAN: Oh, is that so?

ROS: That'll do from both of you!

PETER: It's just so irritat–

ROS: Petey.

She glares at him. He signals surrender.

BOB shifts from foot to foot, feeling uncomfortable.

Now. What would you like for pudding tonight? Lemon meringue pie?

BRIAN: Is it a bought one?

ROS: What do you take me for, you terrible old man?

BRIAN: We had a bought one last week. What was it? Some cakey thing.

ROS: Bob liked it, didn't you, Bob?

BOB: It were lovely.

ROS: Will *home-made* lemon meringue pie do for your lordship?

BRIAN: All right, girl, I'll take a taste of it.

ROS: Very gracious of you. Petey?

PETER: Erm, probably not. Thanks.

ROS: Have you gone off your puddings? Are you on a diet?

PETER: No.

ROS: You used to love puddings.

BRIAN: He's watching his figure, that's what he's doing.
Keeping himself trim. For that housemate of his. Isn't that
right, son?

PETER doesn't react.

They go to concerts together. Mozart. In G Minor.
Who'd've thought it, eh, Ros? Your brother being a
poofter. Your mother would turn in her grave. Nothing was
ever said, but I knew. I knew what sort of a son we had.

PETER looks at BRIAN, gets up and walks out of the room.

ROS: *(Appalled.)* How can you say such things?

BRIAN: Just speaking the truth.

ROS: You don't know it's the truth! You're just being
deliberately cruel.

BRIAN: You're not in tune with the fashionable London ways,
are you, girl?

ROS: Are you?

BRIAN: I know what goes on.

ROS: You know what goes on in TV programmes, that's what
you know.

BRIAN: Ah, well, that's what you might like to think.
No, I'll be getting no grand-kiddies off him.

ROS: You have a grandson. You have William.

BRIAN: Could always get married again myself. How about
that then, eh? How would you fancy your old man getting
wed again? It happens, y'know, men of my age getting wed
and having second families. What do you reckon, Bob?
I could start another family, couldn't I?

BOB: Well…

BRIAN: May have lost the use of me legs, but there's some things you don't need to stand up for, isn't that right?

BOB: I get your meaning there, Brian. *(He chuckles.)*

ROS: Really, Dad, there's no need to be crude as well.

BOB: Fellow down the Feathers had a baby wi' a local lass when he were sixty-eight.

BRIAN: Exactly. Hope for me yet.

BOB: It were a bit of a scandal at the time.

ROS: All right, thank you, Bob. I think we've established the principle.

BOB: Baby died, though. Very sad.

ROS: Yes, thank you, Bob.

BOB: Sixty-eight he was. An' she was only thirty-somethin'.

ROS: Bob. That's enough.

PETER reappears.

BRIAN: I'm just saying, Peter, I could get married again. Keep the old Calder line going. Eh? What do y'reckon to that?

PETER: Excellent idea. An old man in a wheelchair is just what any woman would want.

ROS bursts out laughing, tries to stop herself.

BRIAN: Oh, so you think that's funny, do you? Funny to be in a wheelchair?

ROS controls herself, stops laughing.

Do you think I enjoy being like this? Do you?

ROS: Dad, we know what it must be like.

BRIAN: Oh, you do, do you? You have a deep inside knowledge of what it's like never to be able to go for a walk, or drive a car, or stand up to have a piss?

ROS: *(Patiently.)* We have an understanding, Dad.
We sympathise.

BRIAN: That's very obliging of you. Very obliging indeed.
I am very grateful for your sympathy and understanding.

Pause. He turns to PETER, who retrieves the bottle of wine from the fridge and proceeds to open it.

Anything to say for y'self? I thought for a minute you'd
walked out in a huff.

PETER: I was just having a pee. Realising how lucky I am to be
able to stand up to do it.

BRIAN: You bloody bastard! That's enough out of you.

PETER: OK, I know when I'm not welcome.

ROS: No, Petey, don't say that –

PETER: I know I don't visit very often –

BRIAN: Not interested in us any more. Too busy with the
London set.

ROS: Dad, do stop it. It's lovely to have Petey here.

PETER: Time for a drink, I think.

He fetches a couple of glasses from a cupboard.

BRIAN: *(To PETER.)* I should've taken a firmer hand with you.
Bit of a mummy's boy, if truth were told.

PETER: Yes, yes, have another go at me, why don't you?
Heap all your bitterness onto me.

PETER pours the wine.

BRIAN: I am not bitter! Never once have I let the accident
make me bitter. I've taken it in my stride. I've accepted my
lot in life, which is a damn sight more than most people
these days. Most people want everything life can offer
– and seem to think it's their right to have it, regardless!

Every bloody man for himself. *(A beat.)* I don't want any
of that muck. Will somebody get an old cripple a proper
drink?

ROS goes to the beer crate in the corner of the kitchen.

ROS: Bob?

BOB: Thanks. Don't mind if I do.

*ROS hands bottles to BRIAN and BOB. BRIAN flicks off the top and
hands the opener to BOB.*

ROS: *(Picking up her glass.)* Thank you, Petey.

BOB raises his bottle.

BOB: Cheers, all. Happy birthday to Ros.

ROS: I think we'll wait till tomorrow for that, thank you, Bob.

BRIAN: Here's to your mother. God rest her soul.

They all drink. Silence.

She had such plans for her grandchildren, your mother.
Not to mention your weddings. Both of you. Won't be
getting any weddings in a hurry, will we? No weddings
in this family. Bit late for that. She had it all worked out.
Ros would get married in the local church here – reception
at the Bell Hotel – it'd be the talk of the neighbourhood.
But what's happened? I've got a bastard grandson instead.

PETER: Christ, Dad, this isn't the middle ages, you know!
No one cares about that kind of thing any more.

BRIAN: Maybe they should.

PETER: Yes, and maybe you should lighten up a little
and leave Ros alone.

BRIAN grunts. Takes a swig of beer. Pause.

ROS: Did I tell you, Peter? I've joined an art class.

PETER: Oh yes?

ROS: Just one night a week.

PETER: Well. That's great. Better than stamp-collecting or crochet.

ROS: You're teasing me…

He smiles.

I'm not much good. But it gets me out of the house for an hour.

BRIAN: Probably going there to pose nude for a load of old lechers. Although she could well be a bloody lesbian when all's said and done. Might as well go for the full set.

ROS: Only you could say something like that. Against all the evidence.

PETER: Dad, you really push it, don't you?

BRIAN: Push what?

PETER: Your luck. Our patience.

BRIAN: I speak as I find.

PETER: No, you don't. You speak like an objectionable old bugger who hasn't got a nice word to say about anybody.

BRIAN: Don't you call me a bugger!

ROS: Come on, Dad, it's nearly time for the six o'clock news. You don't want to miss the news. Bob, take him through, will you? I think he's said quite enough for one day.

BOB: Rightio.

BOB manoeuvres BRIAN's wheelchair out into the hall towards the sitting room.

BRIAN: I'll take the beer with me, Bob.

BOB collects BRIAN's glass of beer and wheels him out.

PETER sits, tops up their glasses again. The sound of the TV is again heard indistinctly.

PETER: He gets worse as he gets older.

ROS: He's being especially difficult in your honour. Oh, Petey, I'm so sorry.

PETER: I think we both know that he does his best to find wounding things to say just to assert his position as 'head of the family'. 'I may be in a wheelchair but I'm still the boss.'

ROS puts a hand on his arm, affectionately. He puts his hand on hers.

ROS: *(Seeing he has topped up her glass.)* Oh, thanks. Nice wine.

PETER: Purely Fussy.

ROS: Hmm?

She removes her hand.

PETER: It's what we smart Londoners… Sorry. I must stop saying that.

A beat.

ROS: *(Rousing herself.)* Better get on with the potatoes. They're not going to peel themselves. And these things need washing up.

She starts to clear the lunch plates into the sink.

PETER helps to clear the table.

PETER: Don't suppose you ever thought you'd still be here by now.

ROS: That's the understatement of the year. No. I had my sights set on South America.

PETER: *(Surprised.)* Really?

ROS: But a cottage in Cornwall would have done just as well.

PETER: He has to let you off the hook at some point.

ROS smiles, starts to wash up.

PETER quotes a verse from 'As I Walked Out One Evening' by WH Auden – 'O plunge your hands in water…'

ROS: Is that something you've written?

PETER: I wish. It's a poem by WH Auden.

ROS: Bit of a pessimist, was he?

PETER: I got my Year Elevens to read it in class. They thought it was a hoot. Which illustrated Auden's point exactly. Whatever we do – or don't do – Time is laughing its head off at us. One day we'll turn around and wonder where our lives went.

ROS: I think Mother would have identified with that sentiment. *(A beat.)* I always remember when I showed her that poem I wrote at school.

PETER: What was that?

ROS: You know – about when we moved here. Contrast of landscapes, that sort of thing.

PETER: Oh yes.

ROS: You don't remember, do you?

PETER: Erm, vaguely, yes.

ROS: Mother was equally unimpressed by my efforts. I proudly told her I was going to write a poem a week, and she said: 'You don't want to be wasting your time with things like that, my girl, you want to be out in the fresh air.'

PETER: Ah. Well, that's Mother.

ROS: I felt crushed at the time. No comment on the poem at all. I never wrote another word.

Pause.

PETER: Do you think it's worse to have grand ambitions and not have them fulfilled, or to have *modest* ambitions and not have them fulfilled?

ROS: Well, there's a question.

PETER: Not entirely a rhetorical one.

He smiles. ROS touches his hair lightly, just for a moment.

ROS: I don't think Dad's ever got over what happened to Mother.

PETER: Nor losing his business. Not to mention his legs. Use of.

ROS: You're wicked!

PETER: Well… He's lucky he didn't end up in a mangled heap. Not being able to tell one bit of him from another.

ROS: Don't.

She seems on the verge of tears. Calms herself.

PETER: Sorry. Sorry, Ros.

ROS: I still have nightmares about the accident. Even now.

PETER: Well, something like that is always going to stay with you, isn't it?

ROS: *(Nods in agreement, then:)* Dad's also angry because he thinks you haven't made the best of yourself.

PETER: And he thinks being a school teacher is nothing, does he? What does he *want* me to be?

ROS: I think he rather felt you'd make a good university professor.

PETER: *(Taken aback.)* Really? Did he say that?

ROS: Something like it. Once.

PETER: Why?

ROS: I don't know. Probably because it would've been more of a boast down the Fox and Feathers.

PETER: Oh great. I'm a disappointment not only to him, but to his drinking companions as well.

ROS smiles. Starts to dry the cups and plates. She proceeds to hand him things as she dries them. He puts them away in their respective places.

Great about your art class, by the way.

ROS: Well, I had to do something to get out of the house occasionally. Now Bob's not around so much the evenings get very wearing. He still takes Dad down to the Feathers every now and then, though. Tries to do his bit.

PETER: Tries to get back into your affections you mean?

ROS: Maybe. But it's gone beyond that, Petey. I was never 'in love' with him, as you well know, but he was interested in me. He was a decent enough man, on his own, who'd been short-changed in life…

PETER: And that was a good enough reason to have a child with him?

ROS heaves a deep sigh.

I'm sorry. Don't answer that.

ROS: For goodness' sake, you're talking about William. What would I have done without William? He changed my life.

PETER nods, gestures an apology.

PETER: I've tried to change things too. I applied for a new job.

ROS: Oh? What?

PETER: Don't get excited – only at my school. Head of English. I didn't get the Deputy Headship I applied for in Ealing, so I thought I'd try something closer to home.

ROS: That's wonderful. Just right for you. You'll be wonderful. When do you hear?

PETER gives her a wan smile.

Oh. You didn't get it?

PETER: No. I didn't get it. I agonised over it for weeks, and finally I thought – you never get anywhere if you don't try, and…well, now I wish I hadn't bothered. Someone else got it – someone much younger, of course. And everyone knows I *didn't* get it. So I'm still *Deputy* Head of English, with a line manger ten years' my junior. Stupid, really. If I was going to get a promotion it would have happened by now.

ROS: I'm so sorry, Petey. That's so unfair.

BRIAN wheels himself back in from the hallway.

BRIAN: And another thing. If you ever try bringing one of your fancy-men here again he won't be welcome. I've done my best to be tolerant, but some things I just can't get my head round. OK? You can do what you like down in London and none us will give a toss, but you try and bring that kind of life here and the door will be closed.

ROS: Dad, please!

BRIAN: You I'm happy to see whenever you care to grace us with your presence – you're my son, you're my flesh and blood. I don't approve of what you've become, but we should never hold our hopes too high – that's the lesson I've learned. Don't expect too much of your children because chances are you'll be disappointed. There. I've said my piece. Had to get it off my chest. If it offends you, I'm sorry. But there it is.

ROS: How can you talk like that? How can you?

BRIAN: Oh, so we're suddenly sticking up for little brother, are we? You've changed your tune.

ROS: That is ridiculous –

BRIAN: Yes, we're a ridiculous family, aren't we? Don't know what Bob must think to hear us going on like this. Must think he's lucky to be out of your clutches now.

ROS: Mother would be ashamed to hear you speaking the way you are, utterly ashamed –

BRIAN: Don't you bring your mother into this – you should be proud to be half the woman she was!

ROS: Oh, for goodness' sake! Let's not pretend any more! Mother was no saint, as you well know. She went off with another man because you drove her to it with your constant sniping. And when you found out you went after her and dragged her back, and you were so angry you didn't pay proper attention to your driving, and we all know what happened next –

BRIAN: How dare you! How dare you say such a thing – to me – in my own house! That's – that's – absolute – absolute – rubbish, nonsense, I've never heard so much utter…in my whole life…

BRIAN breaks down, mouthing incomprehensibly.

BOB appears in the doorway to the hall, and looks on, quizzically.

ROS leans on the kitchen table, exhausted, uncomfortable, regretful. She looks up at PETER.

ROS: I'm sorry. But it had to be said.

Blackout.

Music.

SCENE TWO

Projection: Saturday, 8 May, 2010. It fades.

JACQUI, a woman of forty-two, well-groomed and well-spoken, is preparing some finger food, varieties of which are covering most of the kitchen table. She wears an apron over a smart party dress.

The model boat can be seen on top of the fridge, perched on a biscuit tin. It has noticeably progressed, but is still not complete.

Music fades. WILLIAM enters from the garden door. He is twenty-three years old, and dressed smartly but casually in shirt, chinos and expensive leather shoes. Whatever Norfolk accent he may have had has worn off to some extent since leaving home. On seeing JACQUI, he pauses. She looks up at him. Big professional smile.

WILLIAM: Hello.

JACQUI: Hello.

WILLIAM: I don't think we've –

JACQUI: I'm Jacqui. You must be William.

She wipes her well-manicured hands carefully on a towel.

WILLIAM: Yes, I –

JACQUI: Pleased to meet you, William.

WILLIAM: You too.

They shake hands.

JACQUI: Are you called William, or do people call you Bill? Or Will, perhaps? Or, God forbid, even *Wills*?

WILLIAM: No. I'm strictly William. My mother insists.

JACQUI: Strictly William. Sounds fun.

WILLIAM: And before you ask – no, I wasn't named after Prince William. It's my grandfather's middle name.

JACQUI: There's a rumour in my family that I was named after Jackie Kennedy, but I'm not sure I believe it.

WILLIAM: Who?

JACQUI: Jackie Kennedy. Wife – widow – as was – of President Kennedy. *(A beat.)* American royalty.

WILLIAM: Oh, the Kennedys. Yes. I saw a film about them. Sorry, but – should I know who you are?

JACQUI: That rather depends on what Peter may have told you.

WILLIAM: Right…

JACQUI: But knowing Peter, that's probably not much.

WILLIAM: Well, no, he hasn't said –

JACQUI: We drove up together.

WILLIAM: I see. Kind of. Are you…?

JACQUI: Am I what?

WILLIAM: Well, erm, don't know, really. Sorry, I'm probably saying all the wrong things –

JACQUI: We're friends. We met on the circuit.

WILLIAM gives her an enquiring look.

Political circuit.

WILLIAM: Oh. OK.

JACQUI: I was helping with the election campaign. As was he. In a minor capacity.

WILLIAM: What capacity is that?

JACQUI: Leafleting. Ringing people up. Emailing. You know.

WILLIAM: Yes, I see. Well, that's… *(He nods, smiles.)*

JACQUI: Yes.

Pause.

WILLIAM: And are you here now to help with the catering?

JACQUI: Helping with the catering is incidental. I'm here for the party.

WILLIAM: Oh. Right.

JACQUI: And I don't mean political party, obviously.

WILLIAM: No, no. Mum's big birthday –

JACQUI: Exactly. And…to meet you all.

WILLIAM: I see. I'm sorry. I didn't realise –

JACQUI: Why should you?

WILLIAM: I'm his nephew.

JACQUI: Yes. Strictly William. I gathered. I managed to prise a few names out of him in advance. Sister Ros, nephew William, father Brian.

WILLIAM: We don't normally celebrate birthdays in this family. Well, apart from mine, that is.

JACQUI: I'm glad you haven't missed out.

WILLIAM: Thanks. I didn't mean to be rude – about the catering.

JACQUI: You can be as rude as you like. It's all his work. I'm only tinkering with the finger buffet.

WILLIAM: No, I meant –

JACQUI: I know what you meant.

Small pause.

WILLIAM: Perhaps we ought to start again.

JACQUI: Peter's right about you.

WILLIAM: Oh?

JACQUI: You are a very sweet boy. Sorry – sweet-natured, I should say. Sweet sounds a bit… *(She gestures.)*

WILLIAM: Yes…

JACQUI: And you work in the City, I gather.

WILLIAM: At the moment, yes. I think I'm going to lose my job, though.

JACQUI: You haven't done some dreadful deal, have you, and lost your firm billions?

WILLIAM: No no. Nothing so glamorous. It's just… the recession. Quite a few of us are going to go.

JACQUI: I'm sorry to hear it.

WILLIAM: Sign of the times. It's getting quite serious in the banking sector.

JACQUI: Tell me about it.

WILLIAM: Are you in that line too?

JACQUI: No, I'm in PR, but I have a lot of friends in the City – in one capacity or another.

WILLIAM: Which PR company do you work for?

JACQUI: I don't. I work for myself.

WILLIAM: Oh, right.

JACQUI: I am a company.

WILLIAM: *(Sounding impressed.)* Right.

JACQUI: But politics is rather taking over my life at present.

WILLIAM: I try not to let it do that.

JACQUI: Some of us are natural participators. Others not.

   A beat.

WILLIAM: So. Coalition government, eh? Bit of a non-result.

JACQUI: The Lib-Dems were typically wishy-washy in my opinion. And frankly somewhat duplicitous.

WILLIAM: I voted Liberal.

JACQUI: A lot of nice, well-intentioned people did. I won't hold it against you.

WILLIAM: That's very kind of you.

JACQUI: Acquitting yourself well in a television debate is no guarantee of integrity.

WILLIAM: No. But the one does not preclude the other.

JACQUI: I doubt whether any politician who leads the third political party, can maintain both charisma and integrity in the face of political expediency.

WILLIAM: That sounds like a very well-prepared answer. You're clearly a force to be reckoned with.

JACQUI: Not yet, William, not yet. But I like to think my time may come.

PETER enters from the hallway. Now forty-seven, he is wearing a trendy shirt and smart trousers, and has a somewhat nervous manner which he is doing his best to mask.

WILLIAM: Hello, Uncle Peter.

PETER: William. How lovely et cetera. Thought I heard voices.

He gives WILLIAM a hug, which is warmly reciprocated. Then takes an apron from a hook and ties it round himself.

You've met Jacqui, I see.

WILLIAM: Yes. Yes.

PETER: She's a very special lady.

WILLIAM: I'm sure. Yes. *(Light-heartedly.)* And very politically astute.

PETER: Don't get her started. I promised your mother –
no politics tonight.

JACQUI: I won't mention the Clegg word once.

PETER: Everything all right with your mother?

WILLIAM: Got to pick her up from the hairdressers soon.
Everything all right here?

PETER: All under control.

*He starts to get ingredients together to make a stuffing – breadcrumbs,
garlic, onion, olives. JACQUI moves some of the plates of finger food
out of his way.*

We're a well-oiled machine here, aren't we, Jacqs?

JACQUI: Oh, extra virgin all the way. Pete.

PETER: *(Good-humouredly.)* Don't know about that.
Eh? *(To WILLIAM.)* What about your dad?

WILLIAM: What about him?

PETER: You see, Jacqui, what we have here is your typical
family occasion, where two of us have reservations about
certain relatives being present.

JACQUI: Presumably you can hardly exclude them?

PETER: You presume correctly. Though in both cases both
William and I suspect that the relatives in question –
namely our fathers – will somehow manage to put a
dampener on things.

JACQUI: Why's that?

PETER: You'll see. William, could you check that I put the
white wine in the fridge?

WILLIAM: The Purely Fussy?

PETER: You know me.

WILLIAM checks the fridge.

WILLIAM: Five bottles.

Trying to create some extra space, JACQUI puts a plate of food on top of the fridge, almost dislodging the model boat, which she holds up and examines with some disdain.

PETER: And champagne?

WILLIAM: Three bottles.

PETER: Should keep us going.

JACQUI: How many of us are there?

PETER: Six.

WILLIAM: Do you want me to open the red?

PETER: Bit too soon.

JACQUI: *(Still looking at the boat.)* What's this, Peter? One of your youthful efforts?

PETER: No, that's Bob's.

WILLIAM: He's quite proud of it, actually. It's a labour of love.

JACQUI: *(All smiles.)* That's nice.

She replaces it, and instinctively dusts off her hands.

PETER: Oh, Jacqui, would you mind getting the herbs from the garden?

JACQUI: Not if you show me where they are.

PETER: Sure. We need about three handfuls of mint, parsley and thyme.

He takes a pair of scissors from a drawer and leads the way out to the garden. JACQUI follows.

WILLIAM examines the finger food. Samples something exotic-looking.

PETER returns.

Hands off.

WILLIAM: There's enough here for an army.

PETER: No point in stinting. This isn't a peanuts and crisps do, you know.

WILLIAM: I can see that. I'm impressed.

The front doorbell rings.

PETER: That'll probably be your father. Can you let him in?

WILLIAM goes out to the hall.

PETER busies himself with some garlic and a chopping board.

WILLIAM: *(Off.)* Pa…

BOB: *(Off.)* Y' all right, son?

WILLIAM: *(Off.)* Fine. You?

BOB: *(Off.)* Fair to middlin'.

During this exchange, PETER suddenly remembers something, goes to his jacket, which is hanging on a hook or the back of a chair, and checks the pocket. Satisfied, he returns to his task.

BOB enters, followed by WILLIAM. BOB, now fifty-seven, is, for him, dressed up, with a badly-tied tie and a jacket too small for him.

Peter.

PETER: Bob.

BOB: Y' all right?

PETER: *(Not stopping what he's doing.)* I'm all right.
How are you?

BOB: Fair to middlin'. *(A silence.)* Lot of food you got here.

PETER: That's the idea, yes.

WILLIAM: Anything I can do to help, Uncle Peter?

PETER: No no. I'm better on my own.

JACQUI enters, with a handful of herbs.

JACQUI: That's a charming thing to say, Peter. Better on your own?

BOB: *(Awkwardly.)* Oh. Hello.

JACQUI: Hello. I'm Jacqui. How do you do?

PETER: Yes, this is Jacqui. Bob – Jacqui.

BOB: How do.

They shake hands.

JACQUI: Let me see – you're Ros's husband, is that right?

BOB: Not exac'ly.

JACQUI: Oh. I thought –

WILLIAM: He's my father.

BOB: Yes. I'm William's dad.

WILLIAM: My parents aren't married.

JACQUI: Nothing wrong with that.

BOB: No one said there was anything wrong wi' it.

JACQUI: Quite. Here you are, Peter. Herbs as requested.

PETER: *(Intent on his task.)* Thanks. Just put them there, would you?

JACQUI: Would you like me to chop them?

PETER: I'll do it.

BOB: *(Making an effort at conversation.)* Here for the caterin', are ye?

JACQUI: Do you know, Bob, I think I might as well be.

PETER: What do you mean by that?

JACQUI: Do you ever tell anybody anything?

PETER: I'm sorry. Bob, this is Jacqui Price. My…ladyfriend.

BOB: *(Confused.)* Oh. Right.

JACQUI rolls her eyes.

Is Harry comin'?

PETER: No, Bob. Not invited.

JACQUI: Who's Harry?

PETER: Friend of mine. Chap who owns the other half of the house.

JACQUI: Your house in London?

PETER: Yes.

JACQUI: I thought it was all yours.

PETER: In practical terms, yes. He's living elsewhere these days.

JACQUI: You never mentioned this before.

PETER: I'm sure I have.

BOB: He's a nice bloke, Harry. Helped me with my boat.

PETER: That's right, Bob. Well remembered. Came up for a weekend about seven, eight years ago.

BOB: He told this funny story about two blokes in a bar. It were right funny.

WILLIAM: Pa, why don't we go and watch the telly and let Peter and Jacqui get on in the kitchen?

BOB: A' right, son.

WILLIAM: Uncle Peter, I'm off to get Mum in a minute. Do you want me to get Granddad too?

PETER: Rather not have him at all, but thank you, yes, William, that would be kind.

BOB: Bit mean not to have Brian here, on a special occasion, like.

PETER: Yes, Bob, I know. But he *is* going to be here, isn't he? He won't like the food, he won't drink the wine, he'll resent the fact that we're all here in *his* house when he no longer is, but we'll all make the best of it. Won't we?

BOB: Oh, yes. We'll all have a grand time.

WILLIAM: Come along, Pa.

BOB: *(As he goes, aside to WILLIAM.)* Are they – you know? Together, like? Peter and Whatsername?

WILLIAM: Ssh. Come along. You can watch a bit of Alan Titchmarsh.

BOB: I thought he was – you know.

WILLIAM: Alan Titchmarsh? Don't think so, Pa…

They are gone.

JACQUI: I thought you told everyone I was coming. You told me you told everyone I was coming. Otherwise I wouldn't have come.

PETER: Well, I sort of mentioned it, but I wanted it to be a surprise too.

JACQUI: Certainly seems to be that.

PETER: Look, shall we…the food? I've got the stuffing to prepare for the lamb.

They continue with the food preparation. Sounds of the TV are heard, faintly, off.

JACQUI: And this Harry chap…

PETER: What about him?

JACQUI: You never mentioned him to me before.

PETER: I'm sure I must've done.

JACQUI: Don't treat me like a fool, Peter.

PETER stops what he is doing, takes her in his arms.

PETER: I'm just so pleased you're here, Jacqui. I want this to work. I want everyone to like you.

JACQUI: How come he's not living there?

PETER: It's not his only property. And he's away on business a lot.

JACQUI: What does he do?

PETER: He's in pharmaceuticals.

JACQUI: Which company?

PETER: AstraZeneca.

JACQUI: The big boys.

PETER: Seventh largest in the world.

JACQUI: He must be a bit of a hot-shot.

PETER: I believe so. Look, does this really matter?

JACQUI: Peter, you are a very dear man, but you play your cards very close to your chest, don't you?

PETER: Do I?

JACQUI: You never volunteer any information that isn't actively solicited, do you? You like to keep everybody in the dark.

PETER: I don't mean to be like that.

JACQUI: Are you and he lovers?

PETER: Sorry?

JACQUI: You heard me.

Pause.

PETER: Why do you ask me that?

JACQUI: Because, my darling man, it's written all over your face.

A silence.

43

I'm not stupid, Peter. I've known for some time that there's some secret in your life that you're hiding from me. Some grey area.

PETER: My whole life is a grey area.

JACQUI: Oh dear.

A further silence.

PETER: It's all finished. Over two years ago in fact.

JACQUI: Thank you. At last some truth.

PETER: Do you hate me now?

JACQUI: Of course not, but I can't help seeing you in a different light.

PETER: Jacqui, it's you I want. Truly.

JACQUI: That's sweet of you, Peter. You are a sweet man, but confused.

PETER: That's the whole point! I'm not confused with you. With you everything is…clear. I've never known that before. That's why I wanted you to come this weekend, and meet everybody, and… *(He leaves the sentence unfinished.)*

JACQUI: Dinner, Peter. You have a dinner to prepare.

PETER: Will you marry me?

JACQUI: *(Stunned.)* What?

PETER: I really want you to. I mean, *I* want to. I wasn't going to say anything just yet, I was going to wait till we were alone later, but…

He runs to where his jacket is hanging, takes a ring box out of the pocket.

Look. I got this for you. Here.

He opens it, presents the ring to her.

If the size isn't right I can get it altered. I based it on another ring of yours, but that's probably not for the same finger…

He looks at her beseechingly.

I'll go down on one knee if you like.

JACQUI: Peter, Peter…

PETER: What?

JACQUI: Slow down. This is all so…

PETER: It's not how I planned it at all. But it's good to be impulsive sometimes, isn't it? That's what you've said to me before. I shouldn't be so…*considered* all the time. Haven't you? That's what you've said. Well, here I am. The impulsive me. Say yes. Please. I'm… I'm really crazy about you, Jacqs.

JACQUI: Jacqui. Please. Not Jax.

PETER: Sorry, sorry. I forgot.

The front door is heard off, opening and closing.

JACQUI: Peter, look – I've only just stopped being married to Douglas –

PETER: That was ten months ago!

JACQUI: Yes, but that's not a very long time, Peter. To readjust. We hardly know each other, really – as evidenced by this evening.

PETER: I knew instantly.

JACQUI: *(Genuinely surprised.)* Did you?

PETER: Everything changed when I met you, Jacqui. Honest truth.

JACQUI: Are you sure you weren't looking for a way in which to change, and you decided I was it?

PETER: No, no. It wasn't like that at all.

JACQUI: Well, I'm…flattered.

PETER: Don't be flattered. Say you'll marry me. It doesn't have to be yet. We can wait as long as you like. Well, I've waited this long – another few months won't hurt.

Pause.

Please.

Pause.

Blackout.

Interval.

ACT TWO

SCENE ONE

Music.

The clutter of the earlier food preparation is still in evidence. The murmur of dinner conversation from the dining room can be heard. PETER and JACQUI are no longer wearing aprons, and are in almost the same positions as at the end of the last scene. PETER has a glass of red wine to hand, to which he occasionally pays attention, and a paper party hat on his head. JACQUI has no drink or hat. Music fades.

PETER: What would persuade you to say yes?

Pause.

What would persuade you to *consider* marrying me?

JACQUI: I don't know.

PETER: But something could?

JACQUI: It's not a question of that –

PETER: What is it a question of?

JACQUI: It's a question of…gut feeling, Peter.

PETER: So you have no gut feeling for me?

JACQUI: I didn't say that. I have a gut feeling about getting married again.

PETER: When we first met, in one of our very first conversations, you mentioned the fact that you probably wanted to get married again. Because you thought it was worth another try.

JACQUI: Early conversations don't count. They're just skirmishing, aren't they? It's like being allowed out to play again.

PETER: If I could say something to make you change your mind, what would it be?

JACQUI: Oh, Peter, stop! Please. I'm sorry, I'm truly sorry, but it isn't going to work.

PETER: Is it because of my past?

JACQUI: No.

PETER: I'm over all that, Jacqui. I'm not like that any more.

JACQUI: Well, you say that, Peter, but I can't see how you can just *decide* to be different.

PETER: Why not? If that's what you think you should have been all along.

JACQUI: Are you afraid of women?

PETER: No. *(A beat.)* Well, possibly. When I was young. Not afraid exactly. I just got all tied up in knots. You would've got me tied up in knots too, I expect, but now it's different. I'm older, I'm forty-seven. I'm…more experienced.

JACQUI: Forgive me, Peter, but you don't strike me as being very experienced. Forty-seven or no.

PETER: That's a very harsh judgment.

JACQUI: It's part of your charm.

He is momentarily at a loss.

Peter, I've…been through several relationships, with different men – before I was married to Douglas – well, one *during*, but that's another story – and I've had to learn to be – well, harsh is one way of putting it, but I'd prefer to say careful.

PETER: Careful?

JACQUI: About my feelings. About how far I commit myself.

PETER: Doesn't sound very romantic.

JACQUI: Precisely. It guards against unlikely, or unsuitable, romances.

PETER: And am I unsuitable?

JACQUI: For romance? No, not at all. You've been very sweet and considerate. If a little unworldly.

PETER: So you won't marry me, but you'll carry on having a romance with me?

JACQUI: No.

PETER: But you just said –

JACQUI: I know what I just said, Peter. But I can't carry on a romance with a man who really, underneath it all, wants to be married, and who – underneath *that* – has spent much of his life being gay. I mean, it sounds ludicrous, doesn't it?

PETER: Jacqui, many things *sound* ludicrous, but when you analyse them –

JACQUI: No! No, I refuse to *analyse* anything. You're a sweet man, and we've had a lovely time, but I'm not going to marry you – not because you can't make your mind up about your sexuality – I've got no problem with that – sex is sex, and what the hell – but because I am not at all convinced any more that marriage is necessarily the next step to take. Certainly not the next step I want to take.

Pause. PETER tries to take this in.

Do take that silly hat off, Peter.

He does so, having forgotten he was wearing it.

Although I must say it's rather intriguing to be courted by a gay man finally coming out as straight. *That's* never happened to me before.

PETER: And what if I said I was perfectly happy to carry on with the romance, and forget about marriage?

JACQUI: I wouldn't believe you.

PETER: Why not?

JACQUI: It doesn't accord with the evidence, does it?

PETER: Live with me then.

She turns away, smiling, but exasperated.

Live with me.

JACQUI: I have other items on my agenda now.

PETER: Oh, you mean, politics…

JACQUI: Nothing wrong with a little ambition, Peter. And I am ambitious.

PETER: So am I.

JACQUI: Yes, your writing. I know. Well, why not?

PETER: Can I ask you something?

JACQUI: Of course, you silly man. As long as it's not another proposal.

PETER: When you agreed to come up here with me…

JACQUI: Yes?

PETER: Did you really want to come, or were you just playing along?

Small pause.

JACQUI: If I'm honest, you seemed so keen for me to meet your family that I thought turning you down would be rude.

PETER: So you could say that you came simply to be polite?

JACQUI: I've always been a stickler for good manners, Peter. *(A beat.)* Let me ask *you* something. If I may.

PETER: Of course. Anything.

JACQUI: Now, don't be offended, but how did it make you feel when you picked up a man? In a club or wherever. I assume you have done that sort of thing?

PETER bridles.

I'm not being judgmental. I'm simply curious.

PETER looks at her, decides to take the question seriously.

PETER: Apart from the initial excitement, you mean?

JACQUI: If you like.

PETER: Usually it made me feel ashamed.

JACQUI: Ah.

PETER: I didn't feel anything, you see. I didn't really want…
the person. I just wanted some kind of…contact.
A semblance of… *(He gestures.)*

JACQUI: Love?

PETER: I…suppose.

JACQUI: You *suppose? (A beat.)* You can never say the word
love, can you? You always avoid it.

PETER: Do I?

JACQUI: Earlier you said you were crazy about me.
You didn't say you loved me.

PETER: Well, it's just a different way of saying the same thing –

JACQUI: No, it isn't. I think you're very wary of love. I think it
unnerves you.

PETER: Oh, that's nonsense. All I've ever wanted is a proper
relationship. But all I've ever managed is to share a house
with Harry.

JACQUI: You mean Harry of AstraZeneca?

PETER: Yes. Well, I called him Harry. His name was – is –
really Harilal. Harilal Anwar.

JACQUI: How exotic.

PETER: Anyway.

JACQUI: What?

PETER: Anyway we…lived together. For…well, quite a long time.

JACQUI: How long?

PETER: Eight years.

JACQUI: Good Lord.

PETER: It became a simple *arrangement*, though, nothing more. I protected him. His family were – well, you can imagine. Vengeful brothers et cetera, bent on maintaining the family honour. I…looked after him. And looking after someone can often appear to have all the…trappings of – yes – love. But it wasn't the real thing. We kept splitting up, and then getting back together, and gradually, each time, the need we had of each other – to be protected, cared for, cared *about*, became less and less. I began to think I was incapable of love, in any real sense. Which is very different from being *wary* of it.

JACQUI: *(Not believing it.)* OK.

PETER: Anyway, I eventually worked out that for the previous three years we'd spent nearly four times as much time apart as we'd spent together. Actually, it was a ratio of 3.7 to one.

JACQUI: That's quite a calculation.

PETER: Yes.

JACQUI: Very revealing.

PETER: Yes.

JACQUI: Especially about the sort of person who *makes* a calculation like that.

They hold each other's gaze, then PETER looks away.

Why did you split up, finally?

PETER: He had to move abroad. For his company. Wanted me to go with him. Middle East. Far East. You name it.

JACQUI: And you weren't prepared to give up your job?

PETER: Not then. No. In any case…

JACQUI: What?

PETER: I don't think he really meant it. He was using it as an ultimatum. To make something happen. In the relationship. And I…well, I didn't want to feel like 'a kept man'. So.

JACQUI: Such a torrent of honesty, Peter. I'm overcome.

PETER: I can talk to you, Jacqui. You are the first person – since a very long time ago – since I was a teenager, for goodness' sake – who has made me believe in myself. I've spent half my life not really knowing what I'm meant to be. Am I a good teacher – am I a good writer – am I ever going to meet the right person? And I thought I'd finally begun to find the answers…

BRIAN appears, in his wheelchair, from the hallway. At eighty-one, he is frail-looking, but still perfectly alert. He is being pushed by BOB.

BRIAN: Now then, what's going on in here? Party conference, is it?

PETER: Actually, Dad, I've been trying to persuade Jacqui to marry me.

BRIAN: Why would she want to do that? You're not the marrying kind.

PETER: Perhaps I've changed.

BRIAN: Leopard doesn't change his spots, son.

PETER: Then maybe he wasn't really a leopard in the first place.

BRIAN: You've lost me now.

BOB: Are you gettin' married, then, Peter?

PETER: No, Bob. I'm not.

BOB: Tha's a shame. Be nice to have a weddin' in the fam'ly.

BRIAN: He's wedded to his work, aren't you, Peter? Writing that book of yours. That's what you're wedded to.

PETER: That's right, Dad.

BRIAN: Can't pretend I understand it, but at least it's in print.

PETER: Not a complete failure then.

BRIAN: You've made the right choice, love. My son's not for you.

JACQUI: Is that so?

BRIAN: Well, it looks that way to me. Not in your league.

PETER: Did you want anything, Dad, or did you just come out here to be a nuisance?

BRIAN: Came to see what's going on. Got a strange woman in my house – think I've got a right to ask a few questions.

JACQUI: If there's anything else you'd like to ask me, Mr Calder, I'd be happy to oblige, but I think we probably covered most of the basics during dinner.

BRIAN: Maybe we did. Not that I can agree with your politics, though.

JACQUI: We're going to form the next government, Mr Calder.

BRIAN: You'll need a bit of help there, though, won't you?

JACQUI: Discussions are proceeding in Westminster as we speak.

BRIAN: I wouldn't give twopence for the lot of them.

JACQUI: I dare say. *(Beat.)* Was that it? Or do you have another question? Because, actually, I was having a rather fascinating conversation with Peter. He is a fascinating man, you know.

BRIAN: Is he now?

JACQUI: Very much a man of our times, I would say.

BRIAN: Neither one thing or the other, you mean?

JACQUI: No, I didn't mean that, actually. I meant sympathetic, with an appealing lack of male swagger. It's rather appealing.

BRIAN: Well, it's all beyond me. Too old to understand anything now.

PETER: I'll second that.

BRIAN: Least of all my own son. Always been a mystery to me.

JACQUI: I imagine a man like yourself must have encountered many mysteries in life.

BRIAN: And what's that supposed to mean?

JACQUI: Nothing. Just that the more people I get to meet the more I realise that we all take an awful lot of trouble to avoid the things that should concern us most.

BRIAN: Oh, are we back to politics again?

JACQUI: Not at all. I am not here on the campaign trail, Mr Calder. The election is over. Though quite how it will all work out we have yet to discover.

BRIAN: Yes, we'll all just have to wait and see how many more rich bastards we have to bail out so they can have their million-pound bonuses.

PETER: Dad, please. Not again. It wears a bit thin, you know.

JACQUI: Actually, Peter, I'm rather tired. I think it might be best if I go back to the hotel now. I'm sure your family won't object if I leave you to finish the celebrations on your own. Will you call me a taxi?

PETER: I can drive you.

JACQUI: No. I don't think so. Taxi. Please.

PETER: I'll come with you.

JACQUI: I'd rather go alone. You stay with your family.

ROS comes in from the hall. She is now fifty and has gone grey. She is smartly dressed, wearing a party hat, and is slightly tipsy.

ROS: Where's my birthday cake, Petey? Haven't you got me a cake, you naughty boy?

PETER is dialling on his iPhone. ROS pulls a 'party-popper' at him, which misfires.

Oh. Blast.

PETER: It's in the fridge.

He goes to get it.

ROS: In the fridge? Didn't you make it yourself with your own loving hands? Do you hear that, Daddy? Our wonderful chef didn't make my birthday cake.

PETER produces the cake, and five small candles.

BRIAN: It's a bought one.

ROS: Yes, that's forbidden in this house, naughty boy! *(She kisses him.)*

PETER: Sorry. It's a raspberry pavlova. You like that.

ROS: Yes, I do. Thank you. *(Gives him another quick kiss.)*

BOB: I like it too.

PETER: *(On his iPhone.)* A taxi at number 12 Fallowfield Road, please…

ROS: Let's take it in now.

She puts the cake in BRIAN's lap, picks up the candles, and starts to turn his wheelchair round.

PETER: *(Meanwhile.)* … Soon as you can. Name of Price. Mrs Price. Yes. That's right.

JACQUI: Actually, Ros, I hope you'll forgive me but I'm getting a taxi back to the hotel now.

ROS: Oh, OK.

JACQUI: Thank you for a lovely party.

PETER: Going to the Bell Hotel. Yes. Thank you.

ROS: Thank Peter, not me. Come along, Daddy. Cakey time!

She wheels BRIAN off, with the cake. BOB takes a look at JACQUI, gives a hesitant little wave, and follows ROS.

PETER puts his iPhone away.

JACQUI: How soon?

PETER: Straightaway, they said. They've got one that's just dropped off by the caravan park.

JACQUI: I'll just get my things together and spend a penny.

PETER: Right.

JACQUI heads for the hall, almost colliding with ROS who is coming back in.

JACQUI: I'm so sorry…

She goes.

ROS: Come along, Petey. I'm about to cut the cake.

PETER: OK. Look, you carry on, Ros. I've got to see Jacqui out.

ROS: Petey, if you want my advice, go back to London and patch things up with Harry. He's a much safer option. Trust me.

PETER: Ros, you don't –

ROS: You can't possibly have a relationship with –

PETER: Ssh!

ROS: *(Lowering her voice.)* You can't possibly have a relationship with that Maggie Thatcher in the making. She's completely scary. Go back to Harry.

PETER: Harry is living with somebody else.

ROS: Well, you can sort that out!

PETER: He's living with somebody else in Hong Kong. Apart from which he's fed up with my 'What I really want is a woman' routine. Not exactly flattering, to him, is it?

ROS: Oh, Petey, why is your life always such a mess?

PETER: Well, it wasn't! Finally, it wasn't. Two years of counselling and I was finally getting somewhere.

ROS: Counselling? You never told me you –

WILLIAM: *(Off.)* Mum! Come and cut the cake! We're waiting.

ROS: All right! I'm coming.

A car is heard arriving, then a car horn.

PETER: That'll be the taxi.

ROS: *(Suddenly concerned.)* You're not going are you?

PETER: No. Jacqui is going.

ROS: Oh good.

JACQUI is hovering in the doorway to the hall. She has a smart coat on.

JACQUI: I'll see you when I see you, Peter.

PETER: Right. Yes.

JACQUI turns on her heel, and disappears. PETER follows her. We hear the front door open and close. PETER is left standing in the hallway. The car door slams. The car drives away.

ROS: We can have some fun now, can't we?

PETER: *(Coming back into the kitchen.)* Oh, Ros. It's all gone to hell…

ROS: Don't be upset, Petey. She was an interesting experiment, but she's not right for you.

PETER: I asked her to marry me.

ROS: *What?*

WILLIAM comes in from the hall.

WILLIAM: Mum, do you want the cake in the dining room, or in here?

ROS: Might as well be cosy in here, hm?

WILLIAM: Right. I'll get it.

WILLIAM goes.

ROS: And what's all this about counselling?

PETER: *(Shrugs.)* Well, it was… I don't know…

Pause. ROS takes this in.

ROS: Was it expensive?

PETER: Actually, it was rather.

ROS: You don't need counselling.

PETER: No. I'll just keep lurching from one disaster to another. I'm good at that.

ROS gives him a hug.

ROS: It was a lovely meal, Petey. Thank you. And it was so nice you could come up for my birthday weekend.

PETER: Bit of a special one.

ROS: Yes. God. How awful. To be fifty. What an extraordinary thing. Oh, look at this mess…

She starts to clear things from the table. PETER helps.

WILLIAM reappears with the cake, followed by BOB wheeling in BRIAN.

WILLIAM: Here we are. Come along, Mum. Cut it before it disintegrates.

They gather round the table. WILLIAM lights the candles. ROS takes a knife from a drawer and poses. BOB sidles in next to her.

BRIAN: I'll tell you something for nothing, Peter. That woman isn't the answer to your prayers. Her sort will always revert to type. Every time.

WILLIAM takes a digital camera from his pocket and takes a picture of ROS. BOB puts his arm round her. She moves away, slightly.

WILLIAM: What type is that, Granddad?

A beat.

BRIAN: Superior. Ambitious. Up herself.

WILLIAM: You mean she's clever.

BRIAN: I mean she's not one of us.

WILLIAM: Right…

BRIAN: Won't mess about with the likes of Peter. Not for real.

PETER is suddenly close to tears.

WILLIAM: Come along. Family photo. Smile everybody.

WILLIAM takes another photo and starts to sing 'Happy Birthday'. BRIAN and BOB mumble along.

PETER takes the opportunity to slip away unnoticed.

ROS blows out the candles, cuts the cake. They all applaud.

ROS: *(Looking round.)* Where's Petey?

Again we hear the front door opening and closing.

Oh dear. I do hope he isn't going to drive…

She runs into the hall.

(Off.) Petey! Petey!

She opens the door. We hear a car accelerating away.

(Off.) Petey!

BRIAN: Running after women at his age. Ridiculous. *(A beat.)* Come along, Rosalyn. Let's have this cake.

ROS returns, sits quietly.

ROS: I do hope he's all right.

BOB: *(Seizing his moment.)* Would y'like me to stay the night, like, Ros?

ROS: Hm?

BOB: I could stay the night if y'like. With you. Seein' as how it's your birthday.

ROS: You forfeited the right to spend the night with me quite some time ago, Bob.

BOB: I know, but I thought…y'know. It's a special occasion.

ROS: William, talk to your father, will you? Explain elementary female psychology to him.

BOB: Eh?

ROS: A woman likes to feel appreciated for herself, Bob, not second best to the local barmaid, and certainly not just because it happens to be her birthday. Now, Daddy, we must get you home, mustn't we?

BRIAN: Is it all over?

ROS: I think so, yes.

BRIAN: Haven't had my cakey thing.

ROS: Oh, sorry. William, do you mind?

WILLIAM: Sure.

ROS: And will you be OK to run Granddad back in a little while?

WILLIAM: Of course. Here you are, Granddad. *(Gives him some pavlova.)*

ROS: And make sure he takes his tablets. Well, it's been a long day. I'll sort out the washing up in the morning. I'll say good night. And thank you for your lovely presents.

BOB: 'S all right.

WILLIAM: 'Night, Mum.

ROS goes. BOB, rebuffed, doesn't know what to do with himself, so takes the opportunity to help himself to a large slice of pavlova, which he proceeds to enjoy.

BRIAN awkwardly puts down his plate, beckons to WILLIAM.

BRIAN: Take me over by the window.

WILLIAM: Hm?

BRIAN: I need to get some air. Bit short of breath.

WILLIAM: OK.

WILLIAM wheels him closer to the window, opens the door to the garden slightly.

Is that better, Granddad?

BRIAN nods, takes a few breaths.

BRIAN: Nothing like the Norfolk night air. Come here. I need to talk to you. *(WILLIAM crouches beside him.)* Your Uncle Peter…

WILLIAM: Yes?

BRIAN: …is a fish out of water.

WILLIAM: Maybe. Yes.

BRIAN: But he's a good man for all that.

WILLIAM: Oh yes.

BRIAN: He's made us proud with that book of his. Not everyone gets into print. He's done well.

WILLIAM: Yes, he has.

BRIAN: And he cares for *you.*

WILLIAM: I know.

BRIAN: So look after him a bit. I've been less than kind to him. And to your mother. *(A beat.)* And to your grandmother, for that matter.

WILLIAM: I wish I'd known her.

BRIAN: I wish you had, too, son. I wish you had, too. I should have died in that accident, y'know. Not her.

WILLIAM: Granddad, you can't say that.

BRIAN: *(With some urgency.)* Oh, but I can. You'd all have been better off with her rather than me.

WILLIAM: *(Not knowing how to respond to this.)* Well…we can't change things, can we?

BRIAN: No, son, we can't. However much we might regret them. *(He beckons WILLIAM closer.)* And don't you worry about Bob and your mother not being together.

WILLIAM: I don't.

BRIAN: I think you do.

BRIAN looks over at BOB, who is busy eating.

(In an elaborate whisper.) They're not right for each other. But they've both got you and that's what counts. *(More normal voice.)* Your grandmother and I – we had our differences, but we made a go of things. We got along OK. Right up to when – well. It doesn't matter. Sometimes life runs away from you. You think you've got through all the bad times, and then – well.

WILLIAM: Granddad, do you want to – (go now.) ?

BRIAN: Listen to me, William. You've got to hold things together now. You understand me?

WILLIAM nods.

Good lad. We may none of us be perfect, but we're still family. You've got a future ahead of you and you'll be all right. In my day all we had when we were young was hope, but your lot – your generation – you have expectation. And that's good. And I expect you to look after things. A damn sight better than I did. *(BRIAN relaxes, smiles.)* Now, come on. Take the old codger back to Stalag 13.

WILLIAM: OK.

He closes the kitchen door and starts to wheel BRIAN across the room towards the hall.

BOB: 'Night, Brian.

BRIAN shakily raises his hand in a 'goodbye' gesture.

WILLIAM: *(To BOB.)* I'll make you up a bed on the sofa when I get back, Pa.

BOB: OK, son.

WILLIAM and BRIAN reach the hall.

I'll keep an ear out for Peter.

And they are gone.

BOB puts his spoon down, pushes his plate away, contemplates the empty room.

Blackout.

Music.

SCENE TWO

Projection: Sunday 9 May, 2010. It fades.

ROS and WILLIAM are in the process of tidying up and putting things away from the night before. There is a large, freshly made pot of coffee on the table. ROS is pouring them both a mugful. Music fades.

ROS: *(Handing coffee to WILLIAM.)* I just want to know he's OK.

WILLIAM: I'm sure he's fine.

ROS: How can you be *sure*? He might be anywhere. Anything might have happened.

WILLIAM: But it probably hasn't. Why don't you ring him?

ROS: Well, I don't want to intrude if – you know – if he's with that woman.

WILLIAM: You think they might have made it up after last night – or be making it up at this very moment –

ROS: I don't know what to think, William! I just know I may have upset him and I want to know he's all right.

WILLIAM: He could have gone back to London.

ROS: He was in no fit state to drive all that way!

WILLIAM: Nevertheless, Ma, that's exactly what he might have done. Why don't you phone him?

ROS: It's Sunday morning.

WILLIAM: Yes, it's Sunday morning and your brother's gone missing!

ROS: He's not missing!

WILLIAM: Then why do you want to find out where he is?

ROS: I don't care *where* he is – I just – oh, look, you do it, darling, will you? You phone him. Go on. Use mine.

She locates her phone and hands it to WILLIAM. He scrolls through it with ease, finds the number and presses the dial button. He waits. ROS stops working and also waits, looking at WILLIAM.

WILLIAM puts the phone down.

Well?

WILLIAM: Switched off. Went straight to message.

ROS: Did you leave a message?

WILLIAM: Ma, don't be stupid – if I'd left a message you'd have heard me, wouldn't you?

ROS: Ring back then. Ring back and leave a message.

WILLIAM: *(Sighs.)* OK. *(He redials, waits.)* Hi, Uncle Peter, it's Will. Can you phone Mum when you get this, please? She's in a bit of a tizz. Thanks.

He clicks off the phone, hands it back.

ROS: I am not in a bit of a tizz!

WILLIAM: You are.

ROS: You don't have to tell him that!

WILLIAM: Too late now, Ma.

He picks up a bowl from the table.

Where does this live?

ROS: Second cupboard, bottom shelf.

WILLIAM puts it away.

You only call me Ma when you're cross with me.

He goes to her, gives her a hug and a kiss.

WILLIAM: What was Grandma like?

ROS: Why suddenly ask that?

WILLIAM: Something Granddad said last night.
How he wished I'd known her.

ROS: How was he when you took him back last night?

WILLIAM: A bit quiet. Tired, I expect. A lot of excitement with
Jacqui for him to be rude to.

ROS: For once I didn't blame him. Very attractive, but…hard.
In my opinion. So he was talking about your grandmother
was he?

WILLIAM: Just in passing.

ROS: She was a lovely woman. A good mother to us, but –
I now realise – very disappointed in her own life. She gave
up a lot to move here when we were little – well, I was
nine and Uncle Peter was six. She would have adored you,
though. She would have adored a grandson.

WILLIAM: Why did you move?

ROS: Hm? Oh – your Granddad lost his job and there weren't
many opportunities then in Rotherhithe. No smart new
Docklands or Canary Wharf then. So we all moved up
here, away from it all. Your Granddad had a cousin who
gave him a job. Removals business. Ironic, when you think
about it. Do you think we ought to phone the hotel?

WILLIAM: *(Thrown by this change of tack.)* What?

ROS: Check whether he actually stayed there last night?

WILLIAM: Mum, he'll be fine.

ROS: We can't be sure of that.

WILLIAM: You're not his mother, you know! He is a grown man.

ROS: Well, yes, you say that, *but.*

WILLIAM: OK, I'll phone the hotel. Have you got the number?

She hands him a kitchen notepad.

ROS: Here.

WILLIAM punches in the number.

ROS continues to tidy up, or rinse things in the sink, but keeps her attention on WILLIAM.

WILLIAM: Hi. Yeh. Could you tell me if Mr Calder is in the hotel? Mr Peter Calder. Yes, I'll hold. *(To ROS.)* She's checking. *(Back on phone.)* Oh, right. OK. Yes. Thanks. *(He disconnects and puts the phone down.)* She hasn't seen him, but the bill's been paid and the room vacated.

ROS: Try his mobile again.

With a demonstration of great patience, he does so. Waits.

WILLIAM: You want me to leave another message?

ROS: No.

She sits, worried. WILLIAM rings off.

WILLIAM: I really like Uncle Peter, but he does seem to get himself into some odd situations.

ROS gives a small, unamused laugh.

I mean, that whole thing at his school…

ROS: What thing?

WILLIAM: You know – when that pupil tried to seduce him.

ROS: *What?*

WILLIAM: You mean you don't know? OK. Right.

ROS: Tell me.

WILLIAM: Well, I'm not sure, Mum –

ROS: Tell me, William.

WILLIAM: Well. OK, there was this girl –

ROS: How old?

WILLIAM: I don't know, sixteen, seventeen. She was a pupil.

ROS: Oh Lord above. And?

WILLIAM: And she – well, she came on to him, really strong, after school one day –

ROS: Where?

WILLIAM: I don't know! A classroom. A gym. Whatever. Anyway, she does a full number on him, and she's got these, like, suspenders on –

ROS: Oh dear God.

WILLIAM: Anyway, the point is – the point is he doesn't buy it. He doesn't respond.

ROS: How do you know all this?

WILLIAM: He told me.

ROS: When?

WILLIAM: Week or two ago.

ROS: And it happened when?

WILLIAM: Bit before that, I suppose.

ROS: So quite recently.

WILLIAM: Well, yeh.

A beat.

ROS: Go on.

WILLIAM: Well, then these three lads suddenly appeared – one of them all made up like a girl, with lipstick and stuff –

ROS: Yes, yes, I do know what make-up is.

WILLIAM: OK, OK, keep your hair on, and he says stuff like 'We know what you really want, sir – you want me, don't you? – you like boys, don't you, sir? – you're gay, sir.'

ROS: Oh no.

WILLIAM: Like, who gives a shit what he is?

ROS: But it's something he's tried to keep hidden, isn't it? That's the point.

WILLIAM: Maybe. Anyway, he got them out of the room and that was that. They ran off laughing and shouting stuff. Insults.

ROS: But why?

WILLIAM: Why? Because kids are like that. It's what they do.

ROS: But it's meant to be a good school –

WILLIAM: Mum, it's a school. Not only that, it's a South London comprehensive. Nuff said. Anyway, all I was saying was that Uncle Peter seems to get himself into all kinds of weird scenarios. Like he almost can't help it.

ROS: And he told you all about it?

WILLIAM: Yes. But…

ROS: Yes but what?

WILLIAM: Well…we do talk a bit.

ROS: I'm…glad.

WILLIAM: Me too.

ROS: You've seen a lot more of him, of course, working in London…

WILLIAM: Yes.

Pause.

ROS: William?

WILLIAM: Yes, Ma?

ROS: You would tell me if there was anything…well, anything I ought to know?

WILLIAM: Sure.

ROS: Good.

WILLIAM: Depending on what it was, of course.

ROS: No, I mean it, William.

WILLIAM: OK, OK, relax. All is fine. There's nothing to tell.

ROS: Only I do worry about you sometimes.

WILLIAM: Yeh yeh.

He has a gravy boat in his hand. He holds it up, enquiringly.

ROS: Top cupboard, right of the sink.

WILLIAM puts it away.

Do you see anything of that nice girl nowadays?

WILLIAM: Which nice girl?

ROS: The one I met at your graduation.

WILLIAM: Oh, Miranda. No. Not for a while. Kind of…moved on.

ROS: You do still…like girls?

WILLIAM: Ma, for God's sake!

ROS: I'm sorry, I don't want to pry, but a mother worries about these things.

WILLIAM: You worry about absolutely everything.

ROS: Did you know he'd had counselling?

WILLIAM: Who? Uncle Peter?

ROS: Yes, Uncle Peter.

WILLIAM: No, he never said –

The front door is heard, off.

ROS: That'll be him! Thank God! *(Going towards the hall.)* Peter?

PETER appears. He looks terrible.

Oh, Petey. Look at you. Where've you *been*?

PETER: You mean in the last ten minutes, or since last night?

ROS: Since last night. Did you go to the hotel?

PETER: Eventually.

ROS: Sit down, sit down. Let me pour you some coffee. It's still hot.

PETER sits, tiredly. ROS pours coffee.

More for you, darling?

WILLIAM indicates no. ROS sits with PETER.

So. Did you straighten things out with…that woman?

PETER: Oh yes.

ROS: And?

PETER: And I've just dropped her in Yarmouth to get the first train out of 'this awful place'. She's on her way back to London as we speak. No doubt she'll be straight round to Downing Street to tell Cameron how to form the coalition. I hope she has better luck than I did. If you see what I mean.

ROS: You were talking all night?

PETER: No. We had a few intervals for drinks. And to replenish our terms of abuse.

ROS: Oh, Petey… Are you drunk?

PETER: I have no idea. Beyond drunk, I expect. In other words, probably very lucid. Lucid enough, anyway, to realise that marriage is probably not for me after all.

ROS: *(Putting her hand on his.)* It's Jacqui that isn't for you, Petey.

PETER: Well, yes, that too. Why do I make such a balls of everything? I even made a balls of your birthday celebration. I'm sorry, Ros.

ROS: My birthday celebration was lovely. *(With a swift change of gear.)* Now, Peter, you're not to be cross with me, but I want to ask you something.

PETER: Oh dear. Sounds ominous.

ROS: Why didn't you tell me about that incident at your school recently?

PETER looks at WILLIAM.

WILLIAM: Sorry, Uncle Peter. It just kind of slipped out.

ROS: I know you didn't want me to know – presumably because you thought I'd worry too much – but I can't stay silent about it. I'm your nearest relative, Peter. Well, apart from Dad. I've known you from the moment you were born. Why do you always cut me out of everything in your life?

ROS is clearly upset. She holds a tissue to her face.

At the same moment, BOB ambles in, sleepily, still in last night's clothes, oblivious to everything.

BOB: Mornin'. Oh, hello, Peter. Y' all right?

PETER: Yes, Bob. I'm all right. Thank you.

BOB: *(To ROS.)* Any breakfast?

ROS: Breakfast things are in the usual place.

BOB: Right.

WILLIAM: Coffee, Pa?

BOB: No thanks, son. I'll make m'self a cup o' tea.

BOB shuffles over to the breakfast things and surveys what's on offer. Puts the kettle on.

Anyone else want anythin'?

WILLIAM: You carry on, Pa. You see to yourself.

BOB: Right y'are.

BOB proceeds to make himself some toast and tea. This process continues through the scene.

ROS: Peter?

PETER: It was a very unfortunate episode. Some students wanted to…humiliate me, I suppose.

ROS: But why? You're a good teacher.

PETER: Being a good, bad, or indifferent teacher has nothing to do with it. They do it because they can. Because there's nothing to stop them.

ROS: But did you report it to the head?

PETER: Oh yes.

ROS: And?

PETER: And I've been suspended pending an inquiry.

ROS: *What?*

WILLIAM: You didn't tell me that bit –

PETER: It's only just happened. Three days ago.

ROS: But that's outrageous! You're a department head.

PETER: Deputy department head, but I'm still suspended. They claimed assault.

ROS: Assault?

PETER: Oh yes. It's what they want. To get a teacher done for assault. Fired. It's all part of the game.

ROS: You call it a game?

PETER: That's what it is to them. They have no interest in learning anything because that's too boring, too conventional. They get their qualifications by attacking the system. What they did to me is quite mild by some standards.

BOB makes his tea, stirring vigorously.

ROS: Bob, please! *(To PETER.)* And what will happen?

PETER: It'll go to the local authority, and quite possibly to court. The students involved will tell a pack of lies, and even if I'm found not guilty – which is highly unlikely – the governors will dismiss me. They will decide that they have no other choice in the matter because the negative publicity will have been bad for the school – not to mention their social standing – and taking a swift, vigorous course of action will be the best option all round. As they see it. My credibility will be shot to pieces, and I wouldn't want to go back and face the little bastards anyway.

WILLIAM: But that's a complete set-up –

PETER: Indeed so. But what price one decent teacher against the governors' self-esteem?

ROS: Can't you do anything about it?

PETER: Ros, I'm suspended.

ROS: But what about the union? They'll be on your side, surely?

PETER: Oh, they'll represent me. They'll put my case to a tribunal, and who knows? Somebody might believe me. But nobody does, these days. Nobody believes teachers any more. Everybody thinks *they* know best – every Tom, Dick or Harriet thinks they know far better than any teacher how their little Johnny should be taught – and so we sink slowly but surely into the mire of the lowest common denominator, where every thuggish parent thinks they can sometimes almost literally pin their child's teacher up against a wall, and we accept it. Society accepts it. The system favours the ignorant and the self-opinionated. Every time.

ROS: Oh, Petey, I don't know what to say –

PETER: Nothing *to* say, Ros. It's the way things are. The parent is always right. The pupil is always right. Even if he is a lying little toerag.

ROS: And you kept all this bottled up inside you? How could you?

PETER: Could hardly come out with it at your birthday dinner, could I? Bit of a dampener. You'd have loved me for that.

ROS: Did Jacqui know?

PETER: No. Didn't want her to marry me out of sympathy. Not that I need have worried on that score.

BOB is buttering himself some toast.

ROS goes to PETER. Leans over and hugs him.

ROS: I'm so upset. I can't believe you can be treated like that. After twenty-odd years of loyal service.

PETER: I've known worse happen to other teachers.

ROS: But what about your career?

PETER: Perhaps I should have retired with a nervous breakdown – or taken a job at Ofsted and be telling schools to do things differently every six months. The only way to achieve excellence is to keep doing things differently. And to keep setting *targets* and writing endless, endless *assessments*. No matter how little time that leaves for actual teaching. That's no longer the way. It's the assessments that count. And if the Conservatives have their way, Michael Gove will be Secretary of State for Education and we'll all be learning Ancient Greek.

ROS: But you support the Conservatives – don't you?

PETER gives a small, tired snort of laughter.

BOB: *(Coming to the table with his breakfast.)* All goes on down London, don' it?

PETER: Oh yes, Bob. It do.

BOB: Fancy a bit o' toast?

PETER: No thanks.

BOB: Mus' be hungry, 'bor. Go on. Have a bit.

PETER: Honestly, Bob, I'm not hungry. But thank you.

BOB: Ros? William?

ROS: No thanks, Bob. I'll have something later.

BOB: Nice woman that Jacqui. Diff'rent, like.

ROS tuts, shakes her head.

WILLIAM: We're not talking about her any more, Pa.

BOB: Oh. OK. *(He eats his toast.)*

PETER: I'm going to resign.

ROS: You can't!

PETER: Why not? Why give them the satisfaction of sacking me?

ROS: Because you're not guilty! You've got to fight, Petey. Stand up to them!

PETER: I don't want the job any more, Ros.

ROS: But if you resign they'll have won anyway. It'll look as if you're admitting that you did something.

PETER: Yup. But I'm screwed either way.

ROS: Why?

Small pause. PETER makes a decision.

PETER: Oh what the hell. I did 'do something'.

ROS: What? What do you mean?

PETER: This boy was right up close, jeering at me, mincing around like a… Suddenly I couldn't stand it any longer. I lashed out. My elbow caught him in the face. Broke his nose.

ROS gives a small gasp.

Don't know what came over me. Just wanted to…get back at them. Show that I… I don't know. I don't know what I wanted to show. I was just so…angry. Angry with them, with the school, with the whole…system. I've played the game for twenty-five years, I've been a good teacher. I have. But I probably shouldn't ever have become one in the first place.

ROS: Oh, Petey…

PETER: I think I've got to the point where…you know, where you…you suddenly face the thing that's been in the back of your mind for years. I've been sitting in the car. Staring out of the window. And it's actually quite clear to me now. I think I've been wasting my time. All of it. *(Pause.)* I think I'll go and lie down for a bit.

PETER wanders out.

BOB is buttering more toast and spreading marmalade on it, whilst still finishing off the first piece. ROS and WILLIAM exchange looks. ROS goes out after PETER.

BOB looks up. WILLIAM is watching him.

BOB: What?

Blackout.

Music.

SCENE THREE

ROS is resting in the armchair with her eyes closed. PETER has drawn up a kitchen chair to sit beside her. Music fades.

PETER: There's something else I've been meaning to say to you. As we seem to be clearing the air this weekend. Something I've been meaning to say for a very long time, but…

There are always things you don't talk about, aren't there? Things you can't ever quite…

I'm not much good at…saying things. Am I? Not my forte. But. Genie's out of the bottle now. It seems. So.

Pause. She doesn't react.

Remember those trips to London, years ago, when we were teenagers? The parties we went to. Any party that was going. Anything to get out of…here, and…do something. *(A beat.)* They were terrible, weren't they? Those parties. Well, they were typical teenage parties. Typical of the time. Of teenagers of the time. Teenage parties in all their… what's the opposite of glory? Inglory? Things can be 'inglorious', which seems to imply that the noun would be 'inglory' – or would it just be 'ingloriousness'?

ROS: *(Without opening her eyes.)* You're the wordsmith, Peter.

PETER: So you are awake.

ROS: I'm awake-ish. It's hard work being fifty.

PETER: I think I'll settle for ingloriousness.

ROS: I get the point, Peter. They were awful parties. Yes.

PETER: There was always something rather desperate about them. Don't you think? So many young people trying to find a way to kickstart their lives. Trying to find whatever it was that was going to change them into adults.

ROS: Petey, I'm a bit tired for a philosophical discussion.
It's Sunday afternoon.

PETER: Sorry. You sleep.

ROS: I don't want to sleep. I just want to sit here...lie here...
and bask in the sounds of the house.

PETER: That's rather poetic.

ROS: This house has always had its own sounds. All houses do,
I suppose. If I...sit here quietly I can hear the sounds
I used to hear when we were little.

PETER: Can you hear Mother?

ROS: Yes. Can you?

PETER: Sometimes.

ROS: You were her ray of hope. That's what she always said.
You and your cleverness. Her little ray of hope.

A beat.

What were you trying to tell me?

PETER: Oh, it...doesn't matter.

ROS: I think it probably does.

A beat.

PETER: You remember that time...when we stayed with that
guy Julian something? Big house in Kennington. Thought
he was very flash.

ROS's eyes are fully open.

ROS: Let's not talk about that.

PETER: Why?

ROS: Let's not.

PETER: Why?

ROS: I'd rather not.

PETER: Father was an MP.

ROS: Yes, I know. Let's leave it.

PETER: What is it about MPs' sons?

ROS: Is this what you want to talk about?

PETER: No.

ROS: Good.

PETER: I want to talk about you.

ROS: Petey, don't.

PETER: We pretended nothing had happened.

ROS: It was nothing.

PETER: No. It wasn't. It was something very significant.

ROS: I mean it – please stop!

PETER: I can't. The genie's out of the bottle, Ros.

ROS: Will you stop saying that!

PETER: It's true. I've opened up. Everything is released.

ROS: You're talking nonsense.

PETER: I don't think so.

ROS: You're just getting carried away with words. You're being writerish.

PETER: It's more than that.

ROS: I'm going to go and see if William wants a cup of tea –

PETER: Ros. Please. Stay here.

A beat.

ROS: Don't do this to me, Petey. It was years and years ago. We were different people.

PETER: No. That was when we became what we are now.

ROS: What good does it do talking about when we were sixteen, seventeen years old?

PETER: I was sixteen. You were nineteen.

ROS sighs impatiently.

Everybody else was paired off, and as usual there was just us – the two goody-goodies – the sad brother and sister from Norfolk. Just us and Julian. Who was high on cocaine. And who attacked you.

ROS: He didn't *attack* me.

PETER: He forced himself on you. One minute we were sitting around having a laugh, and the next minute he was all over you trying to get your jeans off – Christ, why do you defend him?

ROS: I'm not defending him, I'm trying to be accurate –

PETER: OK, and to be accurate, I tried to protect you. As a brother should. And he laughed at me and dragged you upstairs –

ROS: Peter, please, I beg you. It's much too long ago.

She turns away, takes a tissue from her sleeve. Dabs at her eyes.

PETER: *(Quietly.)* He tried to rape you. And I stood there, wondering what to do. He ignored me, as if I was nothing, as if I simply didn't count. I stood outside the door and thought maybe it was what you actually wanted – maybe I should leave you alone – God knows you'd probably wanted it for long enough – or –

ROS: Not like that! Not with him!

PETER: But then I heard you scream. And I came in and stopped him. And instead of putting up a fight, or being all big and bold, he crumpled. He slunk off like a schoolboy. And you were half hysterical, so I had to try and calm you down. And I just lay down beside you, in this attic room, and held you. And told you I loved you.

ROS: Yes...

PETER: I love you, I said. I love you, Ros. I love you. And I've never told you that again, have I? Never once. Since then. Since I was sixteen and you were nineteen.

ROS: No.

PETER: And I wanted to – I wanted to love you properly, not like that idiot Julian, but kindly, and gently, and... I wanted to look after you. It was always you looking after me, the younger brother, and suddenly it was me who wanted to look after you. Because you needed looking after. You were so...vulnerable suddenly, and hurt, and I wanted to make everything better.

ROS: You did.

PETER: I tried. I tried to make everything better... And for a moment it was. For a moment. For a long, wonderful moment I lay there, and held you, and you wanted me to hold you. Suddenly we were other people and everything was perfect. But then we came to our senses.

ROS: Yes...

PETER: And I've carried that feeling with me ever since. Wanting to find someone who could make me feel like that. Make me feel the way you made me feel. Then. Strong, and powerful, and sensitive, and able to do... anything. That's what I had to tell you. What I've never been able to say to you all these years.

Pause. ROS wipes another tear from the corner of her eye.

ROS: I'm so sorry, Petey.

PETER: What for?

ROS: If I've...spoiled things. For you.

PETER: No. No, you didn't. You haven't.

ROS: I just wanted you to...oh, come here, you stupid man!

She holds him tight. Their embrace is almost too close for comfort. Finally, she breaks it. Looks at him tenderly.

I felt the same, you know. It was the same for me. And I've felt bad about that.

PETER: Ever since. Yes.

ROS: Yes. Ever since.

PETER is holding her by both hands.

What a pair we are. I didn't mean to spoil things. I just wanted you to find – someone. And I wanted to find someone.

PETER: I know. *(A beat.)* Don't take Bob back. Don't settle for a kind of half-life with him. I'll look after you. Now. Just look after you. Be with you. That's all.

ROS: You're in London, Petey.

PETER: Come and live there with me. Or I'll sell and we'll get somewhere else. I'll get Harry to buy me out – he can certainly afford it – and we'll have this place for weekends. Yes, it's miles from anywhere, but it's where we grew up. Or we'll live here, and I'll write here, and we'll get by. OK, I'm not really a proper writer, not yet, but I'm going to keep at it.

ROS: Of course you're a proper writer – your book was published.

PETER: I published it myself, Ros. It cost me money.

ROS: *(Taken aback.)* Oh. Well, it's... It's still...good. And people will have read it –

PETER: The point is I enjoy it. Writing. And we could – well, we could even think about that cottage in Cornwall you always wanted.

ROS: Oh, that. That was just… *(She gestures.)*

PETER: It makes sense, Ros. Finally it all makes sense.
Can't you see? If William loses his job he can stay here for a while, or in London, or wherever. We just need to…work out our own way of doing things. Of making things happen –

ROS: Petey, only twenty-four hours ago you were trying to marry Jacqui. Isn't this all a bit hasty?

PETER: It's taken me thirty years to get to this point, Ros.
I don't call that hasty.

ROS: No, but, Peter, seriously –

PETER: I've had maybe four or five opportunities for a real relationship, something meaningful, and it's never worked out. A few minor disturbances is all I've managed, nothing wild, or overwhelming –

ROS: I could say the same myself. I always secretly wanted some kind of…earth-shattering experience, something that would change me for ever, but all I had was a few girlish romances. And then… I had Bob. But I don't complain, Petey. It was you who was meant to be the achiever in life.

PETER: Some of us just don't seem to be cut out for…romance …passion, and – well, let's be honest, it's not likely to happen now, is it?

ROS: You had a romance with that woman. It could happen again.

PETER: I don't think so.

ROS: *(Touches his arm.)* Petey…

PETER: Family is what counts, Ros. Dad nearly destroyed us.
We can't let him do that.

ROS sighs, uncertain.

Getting to know William in London has been wonderful. He's a terrific young man, a real credit to you, and I – I really think we could – be good for each other. I feel he's almost like a... like a son to me. In some ways he could almost *be* my son – *(ROS reacts.)* – I wouldn't ever try to replace Bob as his father, you know that, but – Ros – listen to me – I want to spend time with you, now, before things all veer out of control again... Bob is a decent enough man, yes – well, apart from what he gets up to down at the pub – but he can't give you a proper life. You would just end up looking after him as well, mothering him as well, just like Dad, and – let's just be *family.* You and me. Truth is, when you look at it, when you look at it objectively, I'm...a weak person. I never thought I was, but it's what I am. With you, though, that doesn't matter. Doesn't matter what I am. You're meant to be with the people who know you best – and care for you most.
And that's you. It's always been you.

A mobile phone is heard ringing, faintly, off.

ROS: That's my phone.

PETER: Certainly isn't mine.

ROS: Must be in the sitting room.

PETER: Tell me you'll be with me, Ros! I need you to be with me!

She looks at him, but is too distracted by her phone to respond.

(Pleading.) At least tell me you'll think about it.

ROS gets up to go and find her phone. Before she gets very far WILLIAM enters from the hall with the phone, hands it to her. She answers it.

ROS: Hello? Yes, speaking... Oh... I... When? I see... Yes, yes, of – yes, I will. Thank you. Yes... Thank you for letting me know.

She clicks off the phone, puts it down.

WILLIAM: Well?

ROS: He's been taken to hospital.

PETER: What happened?

ROS: They're not sure, but it looks as if he's had another stroke. He's unconscious.

PETER: Oh Lord.

WILLIAM: How long ago was this?

ROS: Erm – about an hour they said. He hadn't eaten his lunch, and was… They called an ambulance straight away.

PETER: Should we go and see him?

ROS: They advised me that we should.

PETER: I see.

ROS: Oh, Petey…

PETER: Yes.

ROS: I think this might be it.

PETER: Yes.

ROS: Poor Daddy.

A beat.

PETER: The stranglehold is broken.

ROS: Don't say that.

PETER: I'm only thinking of you.

BOB enters from the garden through the kitchen door. Seeing ROS, he takes his cap off and carefully wipes his feet. He proceeds to take off his gumboots and put on some ordinary shoes, which he has left by the door.

BOB: Y' all right?

PETER: Remember what I said, Ros.

ROS: Yes, I remember.

PETER: Nice walk, Bob?

BOB: Been clearin' my head a bit.

PETER: Oh dear. Like that, eh?

BOB: No, no. Got no hangover. Di'n't drink much las' night. I've jus' been thinkin'.

PETER: I see.

BOB: Few things to sort out in my mind, like.

ROS: *(Who has been lost in her own thoughts.)* I'm going to go and get my things together.

PETER: What things?

ROS: I don't know. Bag. Glasses. Things. William, would you fetch me my coat – the one in my bedroom wardrobe.

WILLIAM: Sure. *(He goes.)*

BOB: Ros, I've been thinkin'.

ROS: Yes, Bob.

BOB: 'Bout you an' me.

ROS: Bob, not now, please. *(She turns to go.)*

BOB: No, no, I got to say it now my mind's made up. I want to make a proper go of it, Ros. With you. If you'll have me back.

ROS: Bob, I – look. Can we…do this later? Only –

BOB: It's all finished wi' Gracie. I've been to see her an' tell her. I won't be seein' her again. Not like that. So. Please, Ros. I'd like us to be together again. You, me and William. We belong together. I should've said this years ago, but I'd like us t'be married, an' that's the truth.

ROS: Oh, for heaven's sake! What a time to choose…

ROS hurries out, distressed.

PETER: Bob, I think you ought to know that Dad has been transferred to hospital.

BOB: Hospital? Has he been taken badly then?

PETER: It appears so.

BOB: He were fine las' night.

PETER: Yes, but…there it is. So, if you will forgive us, we really need to get going.

BOB: To the hospital?

PETER: *(Patiently.)* Yes, Bob. The hospital.

BOB: Right. Jus' tidy m'self up a bit then.

PETER: I meant us, Bob. Ros, William and me.

BOB: Oh.

PETER: I think that's best.

WILLIAM re-enters, with ROS's coat.

BOB: Oh, right. But I'd like to see him. You know –
if it's serious, like.

PETER: I'm sure there will be an opportunity.

BOB: Can't I come wi' you?

He turns to WILLIAM.

I'd like to see him, son. Used to take him down the Feathers. We were like mates, him an' me.

ROS re-enters, briskly. She is keeping herself under control by trying to be organised. She has her bag. WILLIAM helps her into her coat. She applies some lipstick.

ROS: William, you don't mind driving, darling, do you?

WILLIAM: No. Sure.

ROS: Right, come along then. No time to lose.

BOB: Ros?

ROS: What is it, Bob?

BOB: What about me?

ROS: I think it's far too late for us to mean anything to each other any more, Bob. Don't you? Far far too late.

BOB: No, I meant – can I come to the hospital to see Brian?

ROS: Oh. *(She looks at PETER.)*

PETER: Up to you, Ros.

ROS: Perhaps later, Bob. When we've seen how he is.

BOB: Shall I stay here, then?

A beat.

ROS: I suppose it wouldn't do any harm. We'll let you know how things stand when we get back, and then if all is well you can pop over to the hospital on your way home. Go and get your jacket on, Petey.

PETER goes out to the hall.

BOB: You want me t' go home then?

ROS: I think so, don't you? I'm sorry, Bob, but it's better the way things are. What do you want with a fifty-year-old woman anyway?

BOB: Nothin' wrong wi' bein' fifty.

ROS: That's kind of you, but…

BOB: An' if Brian is, well – you know – then you'll want someone around the place, like.

ROS: Bob, Dad hasn't been around the place for over two years.

BOB: No, but – this is his house, isn't it? And if he…goes…well.

ROS: *(Upset.)* What are you trying to say, Bob?

BOB: I don't know… It's all got complicated, all of a sudden. And –

WILLIAM: I think Pa's trying to say that he feels he's part of the family. And that he just wants to help.

BOB: Tha's right, son. I jus' want to help.

ROS: That's all very well, Bob, but you can't suddenly claim me back just because you came to my birthday party.

WILLIAM: Ma, that's not fair –

ROS: William, please, you don't know what things have been like here the last few years. I've done my best to be fair to your father – but I am not prepared to bend over backwards any longer to accommodate everybody's – *(She gestures.)* well, you know what I mean! I'm not prepared to be picked up and dropped and picked up again, just when the mood suits. I'm sorry. I've done my best for this family and now, well, now things are changing. And we're all just going to have to get used to it.

She takes out a hanky. BOB and WILLIAM exchange looks. There is an awkward pause, which ROS herself breaks.

I just hope we can speak to your grandfather, that's all.

WILLIAM: He was making his peace last night. Granddad.

ROS: What?

WILLIAM: That's what it amounted to. He told me how he'd been unkind to you, and to Uncle Peter, and to Grandma too. It was as if he was getting things off his chest.

PETER returns, putting on his jacket.

ROS: He never said anything to me.

WILLIAM: No, I think that was his point. He felt he couldn't, somehow. But he wanted me to know. To pass it on.

ROS: Really? *(Half to herself:)* Why couldn't he have said something to me?

WILLIAM: He was very proud of you both, you know.

PETER: Did he say that?

WILLIAM: Yes, he did.

ROS: Are you sure?

WILLIAM: He said it again in the car on the way back to
the home. He was proud of Mum for being a wonderful
daughter, and proud that Uncle Peter finally got his novel
published. 'Couldn't talk to me about much, but he learned
to put it all into his book.' That's what he said.

PETER: Well I never.

ROS: Come along, we've got to get going. Got to be there.
Just in case.

PETER: It's probably too late for words, Ros.

ROS: There's always hope, Petey, always hope. Come on.

ROS and PETER exit to the hall, arm in arm.

WILLIAM: *(Following.)* See you later, Pa.

BOB: I'll be here, son.

The front door is heard to open.

William –

WILLIAM: *(Turning back.)* Yes?

BOB: You're a good lad.

WILLIAM: *(Smiles.)* Thanks.

BOB: You look after your mother.

WILLIAM: I will. Of course.

There is a moment between them.

Look, I – I've got to go, Pa.

BOB: I know, son. I'll be here when you get back. Just in case, like.

WILLIAM nods, smiles, goes.

Give your granddad my –

The front door closes.

(To himself.) – regards.

Car doors are heard, then the engine starting up, and the car driving away.

BOB looks around the room, goes over to the fridge. He carefully lifts his model boat and looks at it.

He blows the dust off it.

He puts it back on top of the fridge. Looks at it again.

He sits at the table.

Slow fade.

End.

BY THE SAME AUTHOR

The Art of Concealment:
The Life of Terence Rattigan
9781849434164

WWW.OBERONBOOKS.COM

Follow us on www.twitter.com/@oberonbooks
& www.facebook.com/oberonbook